James Payn, Leslie Stephen

The backwater of Life

Or, Essays of a literary Veteran

James Payn, Leslie Stephen

The backwater of Life
Or, Essays of a literary Veteran

ISBN/EAN: 9783337056124

Printed in Europe, USA, Canada, Australia, Japan

Cover: Foto ©ninafisch / pixelio.de

More available books at **www.hansebooks.com**

The Backwater of Life

OR

Essays of a Literary Veteran

BY

JAMES PAYN

WITH AN INTRODUCTION BY

LESLIE STEPHEN

WITH A PORTRAIT

LONDON

SMITH, ELDER AND CO.

15 WATERLOO PLACE

1899

[All rights reserved]

ADVERTISEMENT

THE Essays in this volume are reprinted by permission of their respective proprietors from the following periodicals:—*The Cornhill Magazine, The Nineteenth Century, The Forum, The Strand Magazine, The Times, The Daily Telegraph,* and *The Youth's Companion.*

CONTENTS

	PAGE
JAMES PAYN. By LESLIE STEPHEN	ix
THE BACKWATER OF LIFE	3
ON OLD AGE	17
THE CLOSING OF THE DOORS	41
NOW AND THEN IN HOME LIFE	63
ON CONVERSATION	81
ON TAKING OFFENCE	101
TAKING THE WATERS	113
GETTING INTO PRINT	125
THE COMPLEAT NOVELIST	147
AN EDITOR AND SOME CONTRIBUTORS	177
A LITERARY JUBILEE	195
VALE!	219

JAMES PAYN

NO one, I fancy, who has read the essays collected in this volume will feel himself a stranger to the author. It is sometimes asserted that the author and the man may be two unlike souls in one body. I never knew an instance myself; though, of course, the aspects of character revealed in books may be different from those which are prominent in social intercourse. Payn scarcely showed even this difference. The simplest and most transparent of men, he could no more write than he could talk without the frankest self-revelation. Readers, however, may like to have some direct testimony to the personal impression made upon those who knew him. As one of his oldest friends, I ought to be able to say something to the purpose; though I have nothing to say in which my testimony would differ from that of the many who shared my privilege.

What I can say will be best illustrated by a brief summary of his career. Payn himself wrote two autobiographical books.[1] He begins the first by avowing that his memory for dates and details is defective; and I must admit that his statements suggest one or two chronological puzzles which might give trouble to a minute biographer. But he had both a vivid recollection of many characteristic anecdotes, and a skill in relating them briefly and brightly, which more than atone for any little slips of fact. I can neither repeat them at length nor condense them without injury. I am content to say that the judicious reader should turn to Payn's own narrative. It is the main source of my information, though I can add a detail or two which he has not mentioned.

James Payn was born at Cheltenham on 28th February 1830. His father, William Payn, was the disinherited, or partly disinherited, son of a rich man. When thrown by his father's death upon his own resources, he set to work energetically, and obtained the clerkship to the

---

[1] *Some Literary Recollections* (1884), and *Gleams of Memory* (1894).

Thames Commissioners, a post, as his son says, then of considerable value. He lived at Maidenhead, was well enough off to keep the Berkshire Harriers, and was a bright and popular man, compared by Miss Mitford to a 'hero of the fine old English comedy.' He died before his son was of sufficient age to remember him distinctly. Payn thought that he had not inherited his father's aptitude for practical affairs, and most certainly was himself anything but a Mirabel or other fine gentleman of the Congreve type. His personal qualities were perhaps inherited from his mother—the kindest, and one of the most beautiful, of women, as he tells us, who alone understood him, and whose 'pet' he naturally became. That he must have inherited a very strong idiosyncrasy from some one is demonstrable; for heredity and 'environment' explain everything, and Payn's environment was curiously unfavourable to the qualities which he actually developed. No author whom I can remember was ever more distinctly set apart by nature for his calling. Many men have shown literary proclivities at an equally early age; but their tastes have often been fostered by external circumstances. They have been nursed in libraries, or had sympathetic and appreciative parents, or shown the talents which schoolmasters can recognise and encourage. Payn's literary propensities had none of these adventitious supports. They throve in an uncongenial atmosphere. His father, a sportsman and an active man of the world, would naturally be in sympathy with the country gentlemen of the district. He put his boy on a pony and took him out with the hounds. But the unnatural child found hunting a bore, longed for his books when waiting by the covert-side, and would even go as far as to invent a 'nasty tumble' as a pretext for riding home to *The Mysteries of Udolpho* and *Peregrine Pickle*. He lived within reach of the vale of White Horse, where Tom Brown, or his double, Tom Hughes, was growing up to be the ideal of English public schoolboy, watching 'backsword' play, learning to wrestle, and preparing himself to become a prophet of 'muscular Christianity.' Payn, though he speaks affectionately of some boyish recreations on the downs, was so far from becoming an athlete that he learned to detest even the milder forms of the vice. His cricket seems to have ended when he stopped a ball—horrible to relate!—with the crown of his straw hat, and was properly excluded from all 'elevens' thenceforward. A preparatory school to which he was sent at the age of seven was 'hateful' to him. He gained some popularity as a story-teller, though, like Scheherazade, he told his stories under severe compulsion. He was a slave, though a slave with an amusing accomplishment. Even Eton, to which he was sent at the age of eleven, was equally repulsive. The happiness of school life as celebrated in *Tom Brown* was, according to him, a fiction; and he agreed with Thackeray's view of the brutalities of the old fighting and fagging system. Even in those days, I may venture to say, for I must have been Payn's contemporary at Eton, delicate boys could find a public school enjoyable; and I am not quite sure, heretical as the opinion may be, that the change has been so great or so entirely for the better as is often asserted. Payn does not seem to have suffered much bullying. He says that the 'cruelest thing that happened to him' was the rejection of an article which he sent to the school magazine: a premature experience of a calamity not generally reckoned as one of the schoolboy trials. Payn's literary taste might have been expected to recommend him to schoolmasters if not to boys. But his talents were of the wrong kind. He was not, and never became, a tolerable scholar. The attempt to cram him with classical knowledge only gave him a rooted hatred for the languages, especially for Greek. He regarded it with a kind of personal aversion: it was dead, and he wished, as he says, that it had been buried. His inability to learn any foreign language was indeed singular. Some French and German were painfully drilled into him at a later period; but he was never even up to the average tourist standard. He disliked visits to the Continent, where, as is well known, linguistic skill is required; and he looked with amusing reverence upon any one who was his superior in the art. He spoke to me once of a friend who had been able to translate a letter in some unfamiliar tongue, with a kind of awe, as though the performer of so strange a feat had discovered the key to cuneiform writing. Meanwhile, no schoolmaster could be expected to discover talents so little germane to the ordinary course. In a year or two Payn left Eton on receiving a nomination to the Royal Military Academy, and was sent to a crammer at Woolwich. The system seems to have been atrocious. He was made to spend weeks in learning Euclid by heart. He was at first kept to the treadmill so rigorously, that he had no time for his favourite reading; and he solaced himself by occasional escapades which might have led to worse results. He managed to spend his Sundays in London—not at the house of his respectable relations. He went to the Derby, and for lack of funds rode back on a hearse; and, on one famous occasion, he raised the eightpence necessary to take him and a friend back to Woolwich by preaching from a tub while the friend went round with the hat. Somehow or other he got into the Academy, even passing third in the examination, and spent a year there till he was obliged to leave by the state of his health. He observes that, not being a Smollett, he could not give a fulllength picture of the manners and customs of the place. Happily his literary ambition, though not as yet successful, gave an innocent vent for his energies. The army, then, was not to provide a sphere for Payn's talents; and a certain prejudice against the military view of things in general was apparently the only result of this education. The next mould into which it was attempted to force him was the clerical. He passed a year with a private tutor in Devonshire before going up to Cambridge. The tutor was a delightful and courteous person: familiar with, but neglected by, the aristocracy. Here Payn seems for the first time to have been really happy. For the first and only time in his life, too, he showed some athletic skill, and describes himself as 'quite a remarkable proficient' with the leaping-pole. He speaks of flying from bank to bank of a deep lane over the heads of astonished waggoners. I may infer, perhaps, that his health was improving in the fresh country life; and in such pleasant surroundings he even took some interest in his studies. He was thought to have mathematical ability; and I rather suspect that the belief had some foundation. I am no phrenologist: but Payn's head, with the prominent brow, often reminded me of some famous mathematicians whom I have known; and his skill in whist showed, I suppose, some capacity for calculation. If, however, he had any mathematical gift, it was suppressed by the consuming desire for literary excellence. While he was in Devonshire, he began at last to appear in print. His first success was a poem called 'The Poet's Death,' which was published in *Leigh Hunt's Journal*. Some 'ballads from English History' got into *Bentley's Miscellany*; and he not only wrote, but received payment for, an excellent epitaph on a 'gleesome, fleasome, affectionate' pointer called 'Jock.' Then, too, he received three guineas for a prose article upon his life at Woolwich, which was accepted by W. H. Wills, Dickens's sub-editor in *Household Words*. The fee was spent on a pig to be presented to his Devonshire tutor; and he has told us with characteristic humour how the pig eloped during his journey. A more important result followed. The governor of the

Woolwich Academy complained to Dickens of the article, and a correspondence followed which for the first time brought Payn into direct communication with the man whom he afterwards delighted to describe as 'The Master.'

Meanwhile Payn entered Trinity College in October 1849, still with a view to the clerical profession. There, a short time afterwards, I first had sight of him. My reminiscence is trifling enough, but it left a distinct impression, not, I think, uncharacteristic. I was attending a little debating society where we were discussing the old problem as to the truth of ghost-stories. 'Let any one of you wake at dead of night in the solitude of his own room,' said Payn, 'and see if he dare to summon himself three times by name in a loud voice.' I have never dared to perform the ceremony; nor do I in the least know what the proper inference would be from the alleged fact. But I do very distinctly remember my impression of Payn. In those days I was inclined, like my contemporaries, to attach rather excessive importance to success in examinations. Payn, it was understood, was not to win glory in that direction; but somehow he enjoyed a kind of reputation which, if less definite, had a mysterious charm. He was an author, though as yet of humble rank. Now the Cambridge don of those days, whatever his defects, often had a considerable—I will not say exaggerated—respect for authorship. He was, if anything, rather anxious to show that his academical seclusion was not incompatible with literary culture. Payn fondly thought that even the great scholars agreed with him in their hearts as to the merits of Greek. They could not openly agree when he called a tragedy of Æschylus an 'idealess composition'; but they smiled benevolently and, as he hoped, significantly. Payn generally respected such knowledge as lay beyond his own studies; but on this point I think that he could never be convinced. He had one simple test. When somebody published a collection of Greek wit, Payn felt that it was impossible to laugh at these ancient jokes as you laugh at Sam Weller. Of all hypocrisy, forced laughter is the most easily detected and the most offensive to a genuine humourist; and men who could affect to be amused were to be suspected when they affected to be awestruck by the sublime and beautiful. Payn's heresy was too natural and sincere to be offensive. It might shock a pedant, but could only amuse a true scholar. Payn, in any case, was warmly welcomed by some of the Trinity dons. Among them was W. G. Clark, most urbane and amusing of hosts—then 'public orator,' equally at home in Aristophanes and Shakespeare. Another light was the great Latin scholar Munro, who was also one of the simplest and most cordial of men. George Brimley, a man of much literary promise, was librarian of Trinity, and a contributor to the *Spectator*. He afterwards showed his taste by an enthusiastic panegyric upon Tennyson in the *Cambridge Essays*; and he now praised a little volume of poetry (*Stories from Boccaccio*) published by Payn as an undergraduate. 'The review,' says Payn, 'was like ten thousand tonics in a single dose.' He always called it to mind when himself reviewing a young author; and, in fact, it was the first formal admission of his claims to literary consideration.

There were other Trinity dons of those days whose recognition was worth having. When admitted to their circle, I had something of the feeling of Boswell when elected to the Literary Club. I still think that the society was charming, and the conversation as good as I have ever heard. Payn made friends for life, and kept up his connection with the university for a period much longer than is usual for men who do not obtain fellowships. His visits in later years were always occasions for rejoicing and modest conviviality. Here I need only say that he found a specially congenial set of younger friends at Christ's College. Calverley, Sir John Seeley, Sir Walter Besant, and Professor Skeat were members of the College; and the famous examination paper upon *Pickwick*, set by Calverley, indicates sufficiently one of their attractions for Payn. The devotion for that masterpiece and its author was at its height, and entirely fell in with Payn's hero-worship.

Payn put a very low estimate upon the educational value of his university course: the knowledge was not worth a tenth of the price paid for it. He admitted, however, that it gave grand opportunities for making friendships. He had taken full advantage of these opportunities: he had not only acquired friends, but he had been encouraged, and his self-confidence raised, by communication with fresh young minds, full of literary enthusiasms.

Now, at last, Payn could yield to his strongest impulse. He gave up the intention of taking orders: he had no call, or, as he says, had a stronger call in another direction. His education had all gone by contraries. It had been a series of attempts to train the growing tree into the conventional shape; the tree had refused to obey, and perhaps only shot out more vigorously into forbidden forms. That might possibly be a kindness in disguise, though not a kindness for which the recipient could be grateful. It had certain effects upon Payn's intellectual position. He took himself to be a 'radical,' as the name was understood in those days. It implies something very different now. He shared, at any rate, the radical antipathies to the forces by which he had declined to be moulded: to the 'barbarian' type—in Matthew Arnold's phrase: the sporting, athletic, rough squirearchy, whose tastes were reflected in the public school system and the military and ecclesiastical embodiments of the same spirit. He was a bit of a 'Bohemian': not as indifferent to morality, but as resenting dress-coats and social proprieties, and feeling himself most at home with the free and easy journalist and literary gentleman. His radicalism, in short, was that which is represented by Dickens, and corresponds to the middle-class sentiment of the period—not to any strong democratic or socialist tendency. Dickens's caricature of the pompous officials of the Circumlocution Office and the effete aristocrats who put their faith in 'blood,' expressed some of Payn's prejudices; and, on the other side, he was equally in sympathy with Dickens's hatred of the rigid Puritans and economists, the Stigginses and the Gradgrinds, and love of the soft-hearted, improvident, and generous Bohemians, who illustrate all the Christian virtues. Payn, in short, believed heartily in the morality of the *Christmas Carol*, and resented any criticisms of Dickens's 'sentimentalism.' Such sneers, he said, were only fit for the 'drawing-rooms and the clubs—the people who don't think and the people who don't feel.' When he wrote this, Payn had long been a thorough club man himself, though for drawing-rooms he had little enough taste; and had learned that good sense and kindly feeling are often conspicuous in men to whom Pall Mall is the centre of the universe. Though in some sort a refractory member of his own class in society, he had too many ties of affection and sympathy with it to be a radical of the uncompromising variety. In politics, however, Payn had no very strong interest; though he discussed the popular questions with his friends at the Reform Club, and refused to follow Gladstone's conversion to Home Rule. In early years, he showed his tendency in his novels—where the wicked baronet of fiction made his appearance; and an article upon his early novel (*The Foster Brothers*) in the *Saturday Review* was headed 'The Bloated Aristocracy.' The author (Sir J. F. Stephen) afterwards laughed over this assault with him; but, adds Payn, 'I was never so tickled with the reminiscence as he was.' A lively dislike for pompous officialism, dogmatic priestcraft, pedantic scholarship, and stiff-backed militarism remained equally marked to the end of his life.

Payn went out in the first-class of the 'Poll' at the end of 1852. He was now fully resolved to take to the literary career, which to the end he declared to be the most desirable in the world. He trusted to it to make his living, and had soon strong motives for the industry which speedily became habitual. He was already engaged, and on his twenty-fourth birthday, 28th February 1854, gained the great blessing of his life by his marriage to Miss Louisa Adelaide Edlin. Of the greatness of this blessing I cannot speak. The union lasted for forty-four years till Payn's death; and to those who know what a perfectly happy marriage means, I need say no more than this, that he made such a marriage, and, to the end of his days, had an ever-increasing sense of its unspeakable value. Payn settled at first in a region appropriate to authorship: he was still, indeed, under the one inevitable illusion of a young author—he imagined that he was to be a poet;

and I may remark parenthetically that if he could not, and did not afterwards, claim that title in a very lofty sense, his verses were pleasant reading, and, like everything else that he wrote, free from any affectation of the qualities which he did not possess. A young poet was in his place at Ambleside, where he spent the winter of 1854-5, and for some time he lived 'an idyllic life' in 'Rydal Cottage, under the shadow of Nab Scar.' Wordsworth was dead, but literature was still represented by the brave and kindly Miss Martineau. To her Payn had been introduced by his and his father's old friend, Miss Mitford. These two ladies were in some sense his literary godmothers, and he has described them vividly and affectionately. They gave him good advice and encouragement. He observes, however, what is clearly true, that he owed nothing to introductions. An editor in real life has the strongest motives for accepting new contributors on their merits, and not because they may be recommended by eminent and irresponsible literary ladies. Payn had, in his undergraduate days, watched opportunities for getting into print, 'as a terrier watches a rat's hole,' and had here and there found an open door. In the first year of his married life he made £32, 15s., and this modest income was quadrupled the year afterwards. *Household Words* and *Chambers's Journal* were his main supports, and he began to publish articles every week or oftener. Leitch Ritchie, editor of *Chambers's Journal*, was in failing health, and presently invited Payn to be his 'co-editor'; five men out of six, says Payn, would have said *sub*-editor. In 1858, accordingly, Payn settled in Edinburgh with a regular occupation. A year later Ritchie went to London, and Payn became the sole editor of the *Journal*. He was now thoroughly entered in the profession of letters; but there was one drawback. Edinburgh had lost its old position as a great literary centre. There were still a few men there of whom he speaks gratefully: Robert Chambers, author of the *Vestiges* and one of the proprietors of the *Journal*, was a valued friend, though his brother, a co-proprietor, William Chambers, was never to Payn's taste. He just saw De Quincey, and he had some acquaintance with Alexander Russel of the *Scotsman*, Dean Ramsay, Hill Burton, Alexander Smith, and others. He discovered that there may be such a thing as humour in Scotland, as well as very hearty goodwill. But the literary leaders of the time lived in London. Then there was an east wind in Edinburgh, bad for a delicate family. The same isothermal line, said Robert Chambers, passes through Edinburgh and London. Still, said Payn, I never knew of a four-wheeled cab being blown over by an east wind in London, as has just happened in Edinburgh. Moreover, there was a spiritual east wind of Puritanism which was still less to Payn's taste. A Scottish Sabbath was more than he could bear with composure. Dogmatic rigidity vexed him; and when his landlady remonstrated with him upon drawing up the window-blinds in his house on Sunday, he felt the weight of custom to be more than he could bear. Payn, in short, could never become acclimatised in the Scottish atmosphere, physical or moral; and in 1861 he was glad to be able to remove to London. Robert Chambers made the same change of abode, and Payn continued to edit the *Journal*.

In London, Payn settled in the Maida Vale region, and there he remained for the rest of his life. He became a thorough Londoner; he loved in the early years to wander through many regions of the metropolis; he studied it, he says, as a botanist studies the flora of his district, 'with unspeakable interest and delight.' He recorded some of his experiences in a volume called *Melibœus in London*, for which he always retained a paternal affection. He became intimate with a large and ever widening circle of friends, especially among his own profession. No more thorough Londoner walked the streets, or rather—for Payn walked as little as was possible—paid fares to hansom cabmen. Payn could appreciate country scenery when it came in his way; but he had none of the passions for sport or rambles on foot which take a man habitually into country districts. His absorption in the profession which he loved so well kept him steadily at his post. 'For the last twenty-five years of my life,' he says in 1884, 'I have only had three days of consecutive holiday once a year.' Year in and year out, he was turning out novels and articles, editing and reading for publishers, with admirable punctuality; and with a tenacity of purpose which suffering and illness were unable to break down. In such a career there was naturally little in the way of remarkable incident. I may briefly say that in 1871 his friend Robert Chambers died; and the editorship, which he now held under William Chambers, became less agreeable to him. Differences of opinion arose, and in 1874 Payn gave up the post. In the same year, however, he formed a permanent connection with Messrs. Smith, Elder and Co. He began to read for that firm in 1874; and in 1883 he became editor of their periodical, *The Cornhill Magazine*. He held this post until growing infirmity compelled him to give up the duties in 1896. Here I may say briefly that Mr. George Smith of that firm was a valued friend from their first acquaintance. Payn himself told one anecdote which it is impossible to omit in this connection. He was accused in some paper of having refused the famous

John Inglesant. He at once appealed to Mr. Smith to contradict the report. Mr. Smith, taken by surprise, was unable to conceal that it had some foundation. The letter-book was produced, and Payn convicted of the blunder, of which Mr. Smith had all along been aware without ever revealing his knowledge to the offender. Payn heartily appreciated the generosity, and was glad to tell the story at his own expense. *John Inglesant* has been so generally appreciated that I may venture to add a comment. Its interest depends upon the interpretation of certain religious and philosophical phases of thought, which were entirely outside of Payn's habitual sphere of reflection; and, moreover, I suspect that, however great its merits, it was not at all easy to foretell that they were such as would command a commercial success—and that was the point for Payn's consideration.

To the world at large Payn was chiefly known by his novels. His first regular novel, *The Foster Brothers*, was founded on his college experience. It did fairly, and was republished in America; but his 'first success,' as he says, was *The Family Scapegrace,* suggested by a casual acquaintance with a lion-tamer, known in his profession as Tickerocandua. This, however, was eclipsed by *Lost Sir Massingberd,* which appeared in *Chambers's Journal* in 1864, and is said to have raised the circulation by 20,000 copies. Payn took his literary title from it for several years, but made his chief success by his novel *By Proxy,* which appeared independently in 1878. To my mind, the most amusing of his stories was a shorter one called *A Perfect Treasure*; but I cannot profess to make a confident choice in so wide a field. Novel succeeded novel with exemplary regularity, and Payn could reckon a literary output of more than a hundred volumes. Few men, he tells us incidentally, can write a 'three-volume novel worth reading under nine months,' —a business-like view which is suggestive of his own methods. To Payn, it may be said, novel-writing meant simply straightforward story-telling; he had no wish to propound religious or social or psychological theories, or to embody a philosophical conception of human life. He never, like his master Dickens, wrote attacks upon political abuses, or aimed at emphasising a particular moral. He was, as he had been in his early boyhood, a Scheherazade, and took, I may perhaps say, the same view of his art as the author of the *Trois Mousquetaires*. Payn, in conversation, was especially delightful in the department of anecdote. Nobody could tell a good story more effectively or with more contagious delight. When such a story struck him as specially suitable, it was worked up into an episode, or perhaps became the plot, of one of his novels. I often had the opportunity of watching the process. I would look in upon him at his office, and be greeted with some quaint narrative which had come in his way; and, naturally, every one possessed of an amusing incident would be glad to find so sympathetic a hearer. Then it would be gradually elaborated. He would write down the names of the imaginary characters on a sheet of cardboard, each at the head of a column. Then the necessary dates and facts would be inserted in the appropriate columns, till a full scheme was drawn out and all points of genealogy and so forth made abundantly clear. A writer who was liable to fits of lofty inspiration might perhaps be trammelled by so methodical a procedure. For Payn's purpose —the clearest possible development of an ingenious situation—it answered, I think, very well; and, whatever limits there might be to his talent, the reader might at least be sure of having a thoroughly clear, bright narrative written with unflagging spirit. In early days I had a compact with Payn that I should review his novels in a certain periodical, reserving to myself the right to speak frankly. I fear that I sometimes used that right rather freely, but Payn took my criticisms with unfailing good-humour. Only once he was vexed when I had suggested, by way of apology, that he had written too hastily. Never, he declared, had he failed to do his best for want of taking trouble. That, I think, was no more than the truth. He did what he wished to do, and what his talents fitted him to do, like a thorough workman, and, without further criticising, it may at least be said that the vivacity, the simplicity, and the kindly feeling which is always coming to the surface, make him a delightful showman for the creatures of his imagination. His sense of humour may sometimes lead him to take liberties with his reader; he cannot always resist a bit of downright burlesque; and if an incident is dramatic, he does not inquire too closely into probabilities. Like Dickens, he hates his villains with amusing fervour; and, instead of bestowing upon them some touch of human nature, blackens them so thoroughly that they are only fit for starvation in hollow trees, or at the bottom of Cornish mines, or for boiling or immersion in lava streams, or for some other of the ingenious catastrophes from which their diabolical shrewdness can never save them. Of course, there is always a charming girl to fall in love with, and a happy ending such as the unsophisticated reader desiderates. Perhaps to enjoy Payn thoroughly one should be thoroughly 'unsophisticated,' dislike vice and villains, be indifferent to pessimistic philosophising and æsthetic refinement, and have a certain regard for morality and decency. But, given those conditions, none of his hundred volumes will fail to be good reading.

Payn naturally appreciated the qualities which had most affinity to his own. He appreciated them, too, with a fervour which was delightful to observe. Dickens, of course, was his great idol. I feel a certain twinge of remorse when I remember a catechism through which he once put me. He discovered that I was unsound in regard to some (not all, I must add) of the qualities which he attributed to 'The Master.' I felt as if I had been confessing to a lover that I believed his mistress's beauty to be deformed by a cast in her eyes. Or rather, I seemed to have given him such pain as a benevolent inquisitor might feel on discovering heresy in a dear friend. When Payn refused to bow before some of my own idols it did not hurt me. Perhaps I am not so good a worshipper as altogether to dislike a little occasional blasphemy; but at any rate Payn's antipathies, and he had a good many, were due at most to a pardonable misunderstanding. He was too much repelled by apparent misanthropy to admit that it could be the rough outside of a noble nature. He hated priggishness and solemn affectation with a heartiness which might blind him a little to some solid merits. Puritanical self-righteousness shocked him even to excess. But nobody could be more cordially enthusiastic about the merits which really came home to him. All who wrote of him at the time of his death agreed in admiring his entire freedom from jealousy. Nothing, indeed, gave him more unalloyed pleasure than to discover some one likely to be a successful rival in his own line. He was proud to have discovered some such writers in his editorial capacity, and did his very best to encourage them and to spread their reputation. His dislikes, right or wrong, had nothing to do with the petty personal feelings which occasionally bias the irritable race of authors. His enthusiasms were as natural as everything about him; and it was obvious that the bare thought of making invidious comparisons between himself and others never even entered his head. His spontaneous delight in other men's merits was one of the most obvious and characteristic of his peculiarities. Other men may suppress jealousy; in Payn it did not seem to exist.

Payn, I am glad to think, had his reward.

Trouble came to him at times; domestic anxieties and sorrows of which I cannot speak, except to say that he bore them bravely and cheerfully. But among the consolations was the steadily-growing circle of affectionate friends. He had known and been on the pleasantest terms with most of the literary lights of his time; and in his recollections he has sketched many of them, and always with a bright and kindly touch. Besides the inimitable Dickens, he had known Thackeray and Trollope and Charles Reade and Wilkie Collins, and others whom we then took to be great lights, though a rising generation is beginning to discriminate and classify. But, as the old order changed, Payn was never left in solitude. He more or less apologises for his love of whist. It was, he says, his only recreation, and gave him a couple of hours daily for relaxation. The apology is quite sufficient, I think; but he might have added another. At the Reform Club and elsewhere it made him known to friends who had other merits besides skill in his favourite recreation. When physical infirmities made it impossible for him to frequent his old haunts, the Whist Club to which he belonged made an arrangement which it is pleasant to remember. Four members went by rotation to his house in Warrington Crescent, Maida Vale, twice every week to give him the pleasure of a rubber. Few men, I fancy, have received such a proof of the kindly regard of their friends. I am as incapable of playing whist as of writing a novel; but to me, as to many others, it was an act of self-indulgence to spend one of the other afternoons at Payn's house. He had become so disabled by rheumatic gout that he could not leave his chair; his hands were crippled; he suffered to some degree from deafness; and he had frequent attacks of severe pain. Like other men of his temperament, he had to pay for frequent exhilaration by corresponding fits of depression; and his health in other respects would have been a sufficient excuse for more lasting want of spirits. For some years before his death his life seemed to many of us to hang upon a thread. Any attack might prove fatal. Some of the essays here republished reflect his melancholy moods to some extent; and yet as a rule his spirits rose whenever he took his pen in hand. Payn's buoyancy, indeed, was irrepressible. After the inevitable inquiry about his symptoms, a conversation always became animated, and to me, certainly, he was invariably the communicator instead of the receiver of cheerfulness. Nobody could fail to be touched by his gallantry. Once, when driving home in a cab, he broke a bloodvessel in the lungs, and came very near bleeding to death. He was happily saved, and next day (if I am not mistaken) wrote a lively account of his adventure in his weekly column in the *Illustrated London News*. His contributions to that paper would give a pretty complete impression of Payn's conversation in his later years. Though they were apparently the spontaneous outflow of an inexhaustible reservoir, he had of course to keep the reservoir supplied: he found materials in plenty in current journalism; but he was also fond of many quaint books, old and new, devoted to anecdotic literature, and had assimilated supplies from a great many sources, not least from the talk of his friends. It was a real pleasure to tell Payn of any amusing anecdote. Nobody could seize a good point more quickly or enjoy it more thoroughly; and this was certain to be repaid in kind, and with compound interest. Old stories from school and college days came up as freely as the best witticism from the clubs; and though, as I have said, hardly a keen politician, he was abundantly supplied with all such talk, political or social, as interests editors and journalists. To spend an hour or two with Payn was to some of us to have the sensations of a hermit suddenly dropped into the London world, and discovering not only that he was in the full flow of actual living and breathing human interests, but also that the most genuine kindliness and warmth of heart may be kept fresh and sweet by one who was not above a keen interest in all the talk of the day. This leads to the most obvious reflection suggested by Payn's career. 'If I were to live twenty lives,' he says, 'I would choose no other profession' than the literary. 'It is the brightest and most genial of them all, and, so far at least as my experience goes, the most free from jealousies and acrimonies.' Yet the profession has its characteristic temptations; as, for example, to superficiality, to craving for notoriety, and to cynical indifference to truth. The problem whether you should do your best or do what pays best for the moment occurs with painful persistency, and too often leads, if not to the wrong choice, to an unsatisfactory compromise. Payn's remarkable freedom from some of these characteristic weaknesses was due above all to a quality which he rightfully claimed; whatever else he might have been, he said, he was 'natural.' That was indisputably true. He had taken to literature as some people take to drink, simply because he could not help it. It was his nature. But he was also much too simple to take his impulse for a proof of supereminent genius, or to set down failure to the malignity of critics or the stupidity of mankind. He accepted the position for which experience proved him to be fitted, learned to understand his own powers, and did them full justice by good, honest, hard work. Payn, therefore, had none of the affectation or querulous discontent of unrecognised genius, and, if he did not aim too high, never failed to do his best within his own limits. He was neither spoilt nor soured, and remained to the last as friendly, spontaneous, and trustful of his friends as he was when I first knew him among his old college chums. It was impossible not to love a man who had to the end so much of the simple kindliness of a child. There was not a touch of the morbid in the man's whole character. His indomitable fun, his hearty dislike of meanness or pretension, and his eager response to every show of friendly feeling, were an unconscious appeal for sympathy and respect. When, in his last years, his sensitive nature was tried by many sufferings, his talk never showed a touch of bitterness; he never said an unkind word; and he could extract a harmless jest even from his own infirmities.

No reader will require to be told how much of this was due to the domestic happiness to which he has made a pathetic, though reticent, allusion in his essay on 'The Backwater of Life.' I must not venture to approach that subject more nearly. I will venture to mention one little incident, the concluding one, alas! of our friendship. When Payn was in his last illness—the end of which could hardly be doubtful,—he obtained some relief from one of the medicines employed. He reflected that it might be useful for a trifling evil of which I had complained. He managed with difficulty to write a little pencil-note to me, explaining the case, and enclosing a prescription. That note, written with obvious difficulty, reached me shortly before his death, and is now a pathetic memorial of a friendship of which I am proud, and to which I owe more than it would be here possible even to indicate.

Payn died on the 25th of March 1898, at his house in Warrington Crescent. Mrs. Payn survived with two sons and five daughters. One of the daughters, wife of Mr. G. E. Buckle, has since followed her father.

LESLIE STEPHEN.

THE BACKWATER OF LIFE

A

THE BACKWATER OF LIFE

IT is a strange feeling to one who has been immersed in affairs, and as it were in the mid-stream of what we call Life, to find oneself in its Backwater: crippled and helpless, but still able to see through the osiers on the island between us what is passing along the river—the passenger-vessels, and the pleasure-boats—and to hear faintly the voices and the laughter, and the strong language mellowed by distance, from the slow-moving barges. The Backwater has its good points; the stream is clear, the autumn woods that overhang the hither bank are fair to look upon, and the plunging of the weir, where all things end, has a welcome sound when the moon shines out and floods the scene with silver. Sometimes on darker nights its roar is menacing, but after a while the sinister sound is lost and it changes to a deep solemnity: then we wonder, as we listen, not without fear, as to what may be upon the other side of it. No one who has once been carried over it can come back again. There is the Mainstream, the Backwater, and the Weir, and there ends the River of Life.

Many of us never reach the Backwater, our journey being cut short abruptly; and few of us wish to reach it. It is, no doubt, a shock to exchange sound for silence, action for immobility. We, who thought ourselves so strong, cannot at first resist a bitter sense of humiliation at being reduced to dependence upon others. There are three ways of reaching the Backwater—by illness, by poverty, and by disgrace—but in the last case many prefer the Weir. Some persons, tired for the time of the stress and strain of existence, express the desire that they could escape from it, and be sheltered and serene (as they term it) for the remainder of their days; but this is a very different thing, when they come to experience it, from what they imagine it to be, and very different also is the going into retirement of one's own will and being seized by the rough hands of Fate and laid upon the shelf.

There has been a deal of nonsense written, chiefly by doctors, who have their reasons for being upon good terms with her, about 'kindly Nature.' Nature, like many other folk, can, when in good humour, be kind enough; but she is also capable of great cruelties, which she inflicts with no enjoyment to herself indeed, but with the most absolute indifference to the sufferings of humanity. Her character, for all her smiles and superficial attraction, is that of the genial tavern brawler who, after grievously ill-using his boon companion, takes him home and tends him, whereat all the neighbours exclaim: 'How tender are his ministrations!' but they forget that it was he who caused the patient to be in want of healing. She does but pick you up—and not always that—after she has knocked you down. To speak of her in this fashion will doubtless appear shocking to most people, but on the Backwater we speak as we find. It is one of the peculiarities—I do not say the advantages —of our position that things seem as they are, and not as they look to be, and very, very far, alas! from what we wish them to be. That

Nature should be 'so careful of the Type' is no doubt a reflection consolatory to the philosophic mind, but we cannot all be philosophers, and it must be owned she is strangely reckless of the Compositor. If one has owed her something in the past, we of the Backwater are by this time quits with her.

There is another thing, among many, on which we who are 'laid by' find ourselves in disagreement with the general voice. A great writer puts into the mouth of one of his characters, a very old and feeble man, the aspiration, 'Heaven keep my memory green!' It is a comfort to him to remember his youth; and this view is almost universally accepted. I cannot say that it is the view of us who live—or let us rather say exist—on the Backwater. We agree rather with the poet who tells us that 'a sorrow's crown of sorrows is remembering happier things.'

We think of the far back time when with strong and supple arms we paddled our own canoe upon the river, with companions full of the high spirits of youth. How we 'put our backs into it' as we made the banks fleet by and enjoyed our blameless victories:

> Ah, youth, for years full many and sweet,
> 'Tis known that you and I were one,

sings the poet, but we did not ourselves know it. We were too happy to be aware of our happiness. We were unconscious, as 'o'er airy cliffs and glittering sands' we took our way, of our likeness to

> Those trim skiffs unknown of yore,
> On winding lake or river wide,
> That need no aid of sail or oar,
> That heed no spite of wind or tide.

But in this body 'that does us grievous wrong' we remember that it was so, with unspeakable sorrow. Some tell us that we have had our day, and should be content. Perhaps we should be so, but it is cold comfort. Others say, 'Think how many of your fellow-creatures are worse off.' What a text for Christian souls to preach on! It is one of the most terrible of our reflections to remember that this is the case; to know that so many like ourselves are crying, 'Lord, help us!' and waiting, as it seems to us, in vain for His reply. It is said in Holy Writ that 'sorrow may endure for a night, but joy cometh in the morning'; that is not our case, but the contrary. The 'dead unhappy night' is not so sad for us as the first grey streaks of dawn, when we recognise that another weary day, all emptied of delight, is awaiting us. 'O Lord, how long?' is then our bitter cry. It is said, and with truth, that the spectacle of the happiness of others should always make a good man happy; but even when, as Heaven knows, there is no envy and no grudge, one cannot but feel the sense of contrast.

Perhaps our greatest trial is to watch the lovers as they drop down the stream in their light skiff, the boy leaning forward upon his oars to gaze the better at his fair companion, and she with down-drooped eyes, but a smile that proclaims her consciousness of his scrutiny, hangs one little hand in the water and watches it escape through her fingers. The time has come and gone long ago wherein we ought to have been content 'to go wooing in our boys'; but that love-making by proxy, with the fruition for others, was never, as history tells us, a very welcome proceeding. And now, the remembrance of what was once so bright and sweet and fair, the parting and the meeting, the glance that was mirrored in a flash from loving eyes, the tell-tale pressure of the gentle hand, the stolen kiss so tenderly forgiven, is of all remembrances the most intolerable. Selfish? Yes; do not suppose that self, though different indeed from what it used to be, with no bravery of pretence about it, querulous, degraded, does not still cling to us: it is only to be washed away by the cleansing waters of the Weir. Yet, after all, we have no envy, nor would we deprive our fellow-creatures of a single pleasure if we could. It is the mere sense of loss, irremediable and complete, that causes our despair. It will be shocking to many persons (who are still alive and in the world, however, and can follow the pursuits they love) to learn that such views are entertained by individuals in our position. We are generally depicted as being philosophic or resigned, just as the blind (God help them!) are always described as 'cheerful'; I do not know on whose account this hypocrisy is maintained.

> Alas! we have nor hope nor health,
> Nor peace within nor calm around,
> Nor that content surpassing wealth
> The sage in meditation found.

But it is not to be wondered at that others should take a brighter view of our condition. Just, again, as in the case of the blind, who are seen at their best in company, and strive to hide their sad deficiency from those who visit them, so when our friends come to see us, we put on our best looks, and draw on our little store of smiles to welcome them; and they give a good report of us to our acquaintances ('bright and cheery as ever, I do assure you'), and never guess that when they have gone the curtain falls, and our darkness is deeper than ever.

These visits of our friends are at once the cause of our joy and of our sorrow. It is sweet to be remembered after social death. Our most tender reflection is the thought that when nothing can be gained by it, not even the reciprocity of geniality, these dear kind folks leave their business or their pleasure, and look in upon us, day after day. The Backwater is not a lively scene. It is always in the shadow projected by the platform above the Weir, and the noise of the falling waters is very melancholy; yet these good souls do not desert us. Nay, there is something in our condition that touches them in quite a remarkable manner. Even those who, when we were among them, were mere acquaintances develop the most friendly feeling, and make us ashamed of our previous ignorance of its existence. To 'kindly Nature,' as she is called by those who have experienced only her good offices, we have, to tell the honest truth, but little to be thankful for; it is to men and women that our feebly beating hearts go forth in unspeakable gratitude. There is one—one—consolation in our miserable lot, that it has brought us face to face with the immeasurable goodness of Humanity. Let the divines say what they will of those who have been made after the image of their Creator; let them heap upon them all the faults of their fallen nature; let the cynics aver that what seems good in them is only another form of selfishness: we on the Backwater have good cause to know that these traducers lie. O Love, that cherishes its object when all that makes it lovely has departed, that prefers to possess it useless as a broken toy rather than to lose it, that slaves for it and sacrifices its all to give it daily comfort, that holds all menial offices as gracious opportunities for mitigation of discomfort and of pain, we know you now as we have never known you before. O Friendship, whose smile has been always dear to us, but of the greatness of whose fond and faithful heart we have never guessed, forgive us for our former ignorance. If even there be no heaven hereafter, there are angels here. Alas! though our gratitude can be told, it can never be shown. There are two words that ring in our ears far more sorrowfully than the warning of the weir: 'Too late! Too late!' We are as dead men, though (thanks to these angelic visitors) not 'out of mind.' We think, if a miracle were worked and we could 'get about again,' that we should spend the remainder of our lives in striving to repay them, in doing the like kind offices we have received from them to others in the same sad case as ourselves. There is no harm in having such thoughts, and, alas! no good.

News is brought us of what is going on in the world—in politics, in literature, and in social life. It interests us very much, but in quite a different fashion from the old one. We are no longer actors but spectators, and, as it seems to us, at an immense distance from the stage. The performances are, as it were, in another planet. Our visitors, with tender instinct, select only such topics as are agreeable to us, and strive to conceal from us the reason—that we are too weak for opposition. But, alas! we know the reason very well. A certain morbid sensitiveness takes the place of intelligence with us, and on the other hand is unsuspected. They are unaware—as, indeed, how could it be otherwise?—that their lightest remarks sometimes distress us. They forget when they praise the weather that we shall never more feel the sunshine, nor breathe the fresh air, nor put foot to the ground again. Again, in their wish to cheer us, they profess to see some improvement in our condition, which in fact never takes place. The best that happens is that the change for the worse, which is continuous, is imperceptible. Ordinary invalids have their 'good days.' With us on the Backwater it is not so; there are only days that are less bad than the others. What is worse than all, some good folks think to raise our spirits by the reflection that we may live for months, and even years, longer. Because they are in love with life themselves, they think that, though in some less degree perhaps, it is dear to us also; they cannot conceive a state of existence in which one's chief hope and constant prayer are to get it ended. Others, from equally kind motives, find another ground of congratulation in the fact that, though the nearness of the Weir is evident, we are not moved by it. They do not understand that one of the saddest conditions to which the human mind can be reduced—not from faith, but from pain and weariness—is no longer to fear the Shadow feared of man.

ON OLD AGE

ON OLD AGE

WRITERS have expatiated upon this subject from very early times, though not, unhappily, from the earliest (if Methuselah could have been induced to send the *Nineteenth Century* B.C. a signed article, it would have been really worth reading), but it is not likely, since so many people have had the experience of growing old, that anything very original can be said about it. If 'to live is to learn,' however, there may still be something novel, since the life of one generation is not the same with that of another, and there are peculiar circumstances which affect particular classes.

To the majority of us old age is merely the gradual attenuation of life; a thing 'like copper wire, which grows the narrower by going further'; the same dish, save that it has become insipid: an echo of existence, which in prolongation sounds fainter and fainter. Unless disease accompanies it, there is nothing to distinguish it, in a very marked manner, from the rest of adult experience. Of course there is the physical change, but this does not set in to any serious extent till very late. The years are not yet come of which we are compelled to say, 'We have no pleasure in them,' and when 'the clouds return after the rain.' The almond-tree may flourish and the daughters of music may be brought low (so far, at all events, that their high notes are thrown away upon us), but we have still what are cheerfully described as 'all our faculties.' We transact all our business, often, indeed, sticking to it closer than ever. We say 'What?' a good deal oftener than we did, and some of us 'No.' (If there is to be but one word left to us, that seems to paterfamilias to be the best.) We like it to be thoroughly understood that we are not going to divest ourselves of our garments before going to bed. We even still take our pleasures, though more sadly; they may have lost their zest, but something remains; there is the feast, though it is the second day's feast; the joints have already become hashes, but the day of cold mutton is still afar off.

Moralists and philosophers have done their best, when they have themselves reached that time of life, to eulogise 'old age'; but they do not deceive even the young. ('These old gentlemen,' says Youth, with its callow cynicism, 'are Foxes who have lost their tails.') They have done the same thing with poverty, and with the same ill-success. It has had no exhilarating effect upon poor people. The reasons why old men have written in praise of old age are not far to seek: they say with Johnson, 'Do not let us discourage one another.' They are in for it, and they make the best of it; it is not well to cry stinking fish. Moreover, there is a natural tendency among well-principled persons to make light of the ills of humanity; they fancy they are paying a compliment to Providence, and perhaps even conciliating it. There are many old men who say, and quite truthfully, that they would not be young again if they could; but what they mean is not, of course, that they would not exchange weakness for strength, and disillusion for hope, but that they have no desire to live their life over again. The clinging to existence that we so often see in even very old men does not arise from love of it. Pope, sitting by Sir Godfrey Kneller's deathbed, and finding him much dispirited, told him he had been a good man, and would doubtless go to heaven. 'Ah, my good friend,' was the deplorable but pathetic reply, 'I wish God would let me stay at Whitton.' It was not, however, the attractions of Whitton that he had in his mind.

When old men ape young ones they afford a sad, and in fact rather a gruesome, spectacle, like that of a death's-head moth fluttering among butterflies; but it does not often happen. Their efforts to rival them in ordinary transactions are plucky endeavours to go on with the battle of life; not to throw up the sponge before they are compelled. Their ardour for work is sometimes excessive; indeed, in some cases they are seized with a desire for gain, which under the circumstances looks very like madness; but they are privately conscious of a sad falling-off in promptitude; their judgment may be as good as ever, but their intellectual motions are tardy. Those with whom they were wont to consult are often no longer with them; they have become isolated. 'Remote, unfriended, melancholy, slow,' is a line very appropriate to their condition. It seems curious that Shakespeare should have mentioned 'troops of friends' as accompaniments of old age. This statement is only true as regards those who have the gift of exciting personal attachment: the longer they live the larger is the number of those attracted to them; but with the vast majority of mankind, friendships are made in youth, but afterwards by no means easily, and therefore when men come to be old they have only their contemporaries, a small and dwindling 'troop,' whom they can call their friends.

Perhaps the best part of old age is its sense of proportion, which enables us to estimate misfortunes, or what seem to be such, at their true value. We have lived to recognise some of them as blessings in disguise; and at all events they do not take such exaggerated forms in that quiet atmosphere as they were wont to do in the changeful cloudland of youth. We also know by experience how soon most of them 'blow over.' There is, however, one exception—that of death. When an old man is robbed, for example, of the bride of his youth, the being who has cheered his path from manhood, and in whom alone he has always found sympathy, the blow is fatal, not of necessity (alas!) to his life, but to all that made it, as it seems to him, worth living. It is said, indeed, that such a loss is rendered less severe to old men because they will soon be united to the object of their affections:

> Gone for a minute, my son, from this room into the next;
> I too shall go in a minute. What time have I to be vext?

But to most of us this is but cold comfort; it may happen, but it also may not; there is no direct assurance of it, even for the most pious; and at the best, how weak is belief compared with certainty, the meeting we hope for beside the loss we know! Tennyson, it is true, affirms that death does not harrow the feelings of the old as of the young. 'The Grandmother' tells us that the time when she could have wept with the best has long gone by; but this poor lady was exceptionally old, and the loss she could not weep for was not that of a life companion.

The man we are all best acquainted with—Dr. Johnson—enjoyed himself in old age to the full. But he had had no enjoyment previously. Prosperity had been unknown to him till middle age had passed away. His society was more sought, his conversation (or what did duty for it) more prized, his wit and wisdom more welcomed, after his grand climacteric than before it. This no doubt caused him to take too rose-coloured a view of old age. When the Bishop of St. Asaph observed that an old man must lose faster than he gets, Johnson replied, 'I think not, if he exerts himself.' Whereupon his Lordship was discreetly silent. The Doctor says again, 'There is nothing of the old man in my conversation,' which was true enough as regards its intelligence, but not the nature of it, which was essentially mature and consummate. In his heart he knew perfectly well what is amiss in our late autumn, and how the disease of 'anno domini' had begun to tell upon him. When Boswell, as usual, assenting too readily to his patron's views, expressed a wish to experience old age, the Doctor was much irritated, and thundered out: 'What, would you have decreptitude?'

The difference between youth and age as regards the conduct towards us of the other sex has been plaintively expressed: 'When I was young my civilities were taken as protestations of love; but now my protestations of love are taken as civilities.'

As a rule the poets, though they have a bad reputation for it, do not, when their hair is grey, philander even in verse, and have no illusions as to the undesirableness of growing old, under however favourable circumstances.

> What are myrtle and wreaths to the brow that is wrinkled?
> 'Tis like a dead flower with Maydew besprinkled.
> The myrtle and ivy of sweet two-and-twenty,
> Are worth all your laurels, however so plenty.

Rogers, who was often complimented on being a fine old man, used acidly to reply, 'There is no such thing, sir, as a fine old man.'

A less known but not less admirable writer has, however, given us a description of one who may well be called so:

If he wears his own hair, it is white, in spite of his favourite grandson, who used to get on the chair behind him, and pull the silver hairs out, ten years ago. If he is bald at top, the hairdresser, hovering and breathing about him like a second youth, takes care to give the bald place as much powder as the covered; in order that he may convey to the sensorium within a pleasing indistinctness of idea respecting the exact limits of skin and hair. He is very clean and neat; and, in warm weather, is proud of opening his waistcoat half-way down, and letting so much of his frill be seen, in order to show his hardiness as well as taste.

. . . .

In his pockets are two handkerchiefs (one for the neck at night-time), his spectacles, and his pocket-book. The pocket-book, among other things, contains a receipt for a cough, and some verses cut out of an odd sheet of an old magazine, on the lovely Duchess of A., beginning:

'When beauteous Mira walks the plain.'

. . . .

Ranelagh was a noble place! Such taste, such elegance, such beauty! There was the Duchess of A., the finest woman in England, Sir; and Mrs. L., a mighty fine creature; and Lady Susan what's-her-name, that had that unfortunate affair with Sir Charles. Sir, they came swimming by you like the swans.

. . . .

He calls favourite young ladies by their Christian names,

however slightly acquainted with them; and has a privilege of saluting all brides, mothers, and indeed every species of lady, on the least holiday occasion. If the husband, for instance, has met with a piece of luck, he instantly moves forward, and gravely kisses the wife on the cheek. The wife then says, 'My niece, sir, from the country'; and he kisses the niece. The niece seeing her cousin biting her lips at the joke, says, 'My cousin Harriet, sir,' and he kisses the cousin.

With the exception of a falling-off in quickness of the mental powers, partly compensated for by their greater maturity, and of some alteration in the emotions, old age, as we have said, is generally but a prolongation of the past; but there are not a few cases when, in addition to the weight of years, chronic ill-health or accident withdraws us altogether from active life, a circumstance which, though inconvenient and deplorable, is not without its advantages, immaterial indeed, but by no means unimportant. In the first place, it bestows leisure before the period when the waning of the mind renders it compulsory; like a spectator who watches a vast procession from some secure and retired spot, such persons have an unusual opportunity of looking at life from the outside. They are in the world, but no longer of it, and regard it with dispassionate view. The most ordinary and simple pleasures, such as are enjoyed by the humblest, are denied to them. If the test of humanity is that of walking erect upon the earth, they have fallen below even that standard. Their feet will never brush the dew upon the upland lawn, or linger beside sea or river; Nature, save so much of it as can be seen from a window, is henceforth hidden from them; it is sad and strange to reflect that, if ever again they behold its beauties, it will be in another world. Will there be woods and streams, they wonder, there, and what we falsely call 'the eternal' hills? 'Wet or dry' is a phrase that has no more significance to them; they will not feel again the soft-falling summer rain, nor the cheerful sunshine, nor see the wave pass over the wheat, nor the shadows across the pool. The value of these treasures of sight is only known to him who has lost them; he may not have been one addicted to outdoor pursuits, or specially attracted by the country, but the thought that they are denied to him is a very bitter one; one may be fond of home, yet resent being a captive to it, and still more to a single room, or perhaps even an armchair. No one who is not helpless can understand the misery of helplessness; it is a degradation only to be compared with disgrace, a humiliation unspeakable, and not to be mitigated (nay, rather otherwise) by the tenderest of ministrants. What is one of its worst features is the effect it has upon the nerves; movement has become the associate of danger, and is therefore abhorrent, and the stiller we are, the greater is our likeness to death.

We do, indeed, belong less to the living than the dead, and the familiarity we lose with the one is transferred to the other. That is one of the good sides (for it has many facets) of chronic invalidism: we look on both worlds with equanimity; not, of course, with indifference—far from it—but with neither expectation nor tremor; we have done with those emotions. Another cause of congratulation is the absence of rivalry. For all races, whether for fame, or place, or fortune, we are 'scratched'; there is now no reason why our neighbours should not wish us well. They have, of course, become no less in our eyes—indeed, in some ways they loom larger, or rather it is we who have grown more insignificant—yet we regard them much as a human observer watches the inhabitants of an anthill. What industry, what excitement, what ceaseless toil! How strange is the reflection that we ourselves once painfully pulled about those sticks and straws, and went over and over again that uneven ground! We feel, however, no element of contempt for such labours, but, on the contrary, a sympathetic solicitude. We take generally a pleasure in the assiduity and success of our fellow-creatures that was before unknown to us; it is the substitute for our own pleasure. If we had the power we would be a little Providence to them. People come to us confidingly for advice, feeling sure that it will be disinterested, and with an instinctive conviction that we cannot be ill-disposed towards them; besides, we have more time for thinking than other folks, and (alas!) we are always at home to everybody. We are not quite useless even yet. 'They also serve who only stand and wait'; and when we can't stand we can still sit and serve—a little.

On the other hand, our enemies—and who is without them?—no longer annoy us. Indeed, they have ceased reviling; to them we are as dead men, 'out of mind,' to whom the proverb *De mortuis* applies. And our friends are twice our friends. No one who is not 'laid by' can understand the depths of human sympathy. Even our acquaintances become our friends, and the least soft-hearted of visitors murmurs to himself, 'Poor soul!' or perhaps (with equal commiseration), 'Poor devil!' What is most curious is the interest, if we have in any way become known to the public at large, complete strangers take in our physical and mental condition. If prescriptions could cure us we should be in rude health indeed. The materials are sometimes a little difficult to procure. I have seen a letter from New Zealand recommending an old gentleman suffering from rheumatic gout to bathe in whales. In that island whales, it seems, are occasionally thrown up on the seashore, when rheumatic patients hasten to lie in them during the progress of their evisceration for purposes of commerce. The extreme rarity of whales upon the Thames Embankment seems to have been unknown to the writer. Some correspondents give most excellent sanitary advice, but too late for its practical application. An aged poet who had lost the use of his limbs was exhorted by an admirer to dig, 'even if it were but in his back garden,' for an hour or two every morning before breakfast; all that was wanted, he was assured, for complete recovery was 'profuse perspiration followed by a healthy glow.'

Sometimes—though, it must be added, very rarely—these communications are not so friendly; the occasion of a writer's retirement and inferred secession from the world of letters is taken advantage of to remind him of his moral misdemeanours.

A friend of mine, whose literary effusions had been singularly blameless, had on one occasion humorously commented on a eulogium delivered by a foreigner in high position, on the complete absence among the upper classes in England of anything approaching to bad language. He said that he had stayed in many great houses, and mingled with persons of all ages, from none of whom had he heard one 'cursory expression.' It was well known, my friend had written, that this witness to character was, unhappily, very deaf; nor would it be likely that in the presence of an alien of such high position strong language would be indulged in by anybody. It was very true that English gentlemen did not express themselves with the unnecessary vigour they used in the last century, but he feared that the statement that 'a big, big D' is never indulged in must be substituted for Mr. Gilbert's well-known phrase of 'hardly ever.' He went on to quote the remark of the American humorist, that when a person, however respectable, trod with his stockinged foot upon 'the business end' of a tin-tack, he rarely confined himself to saying 'Dear me!' There was nothing in what my friend wrote upon the subject but the most harmless badinage, far less the slightest approval of bad language, yet, when in his sere and yellow leaf he had to resign active literary employment, he received the following communication:—

Sir, a judgment has fallen upon you at last, as it is fitting it should fall upon those who use, and advocate the use of, blasphemous and disgusting language. You have written, that even well-principled persons are wont to indulge in it on very small provocation. [This refers to the tin-tack.] To you and your pothouse companions [the society frequented by my poor friend was quite painfully respectable] 'big D's,' as you call them, may be common enough, but, let me tell you, in Christian families they are utterly unknown. Perhaps, however, it is but natural that persons of your description should cultivate the sort of language that will no doubt be spoken hereafter in that place to which you are (I hear) hastening with rapid strides.

Here followed the writer's name and address, which, strange to say, was not a lunatic asylum.

It is fair to add that such communications are very exceptional; but correspondents who concern themselves with the spiritual condition of persons we have in our mind—old men who are known to have withdrawn from work, no matter what, so that they have made more or less mark in it—are numerous. Of the man himself, his habits, his beliefs, they know absolutely nothing, but hearing that he is withdrawn from the world, they write to express their hope that he has his thoughts fixed on the next one. These persons are by no means of one creed, and as each one is certain of his own being the right one, their expostulations and adjurations put those who wish to please them in an embarrassing position.

If the correspondence concerning this matter addressed to people who have but very modest claims to public recognition was to be published, it would be pronounced incredible; what it must be in the case of the more distinguished individuals who have retired from business is beyond the imagination to picture.

The majority of these good soul-Samaritans, as they may be termed, are alarmed for the future of their unknown friend. Their view of it is not rose-coloured for the majority of their acquaintances, but for him it is flame-coloured. The fate which they apparently expect for nine-tenths of their fellow-creatures is similar to that which the late King of Benin was wont to inflict upon any one who chanced to displease him, save that his victim had not to endure it for all eternity. These apprehensions are usually expressed by ladies, and evidently kind ones. One can fancy their light-blue eyes growing tender over drowning flies, but they regard the horrible fate of which they write with the most extraordinary equanimity, not, to do them justice, because it is only going to happen to other people, but because, they say, it has been so decreed. That being the case, they have calmly adopted it, under the amazing impression that it is a branch—and the most important branch—of Christianity; they would be amazed and surprised if you informed them that it belonged to a much older religion, known as devil-worship. If the poor gentleman on whom they fasten—or let us say alight, for they wish to do him nothing but good—is so ill-advised as to question these pronouncements, he is lost indeed. I knew one who mildly replied that he feared his disposition was too hopeful — that cheerfulness would break in and dispel these gloomy anticipations. 'But, my dear friend,' replied his correspondent, '*we* are cheerful; *we* have our jokes, and enjoy ourselves as much as anybody.' Then my friend lost his temper. 'In that case,' he rejoined, 'you ought to be ashamed of yourselves. How can you smile—much less laugh—when you believe that half the people with whom you mingle are doomed to everlasting fire? If you felt they were sentenced to be hanged it would make you serious enough, yet you eat and drink with them, under these far more deplorable circumstances, without any check on appetite. The simple explanation of the matter is that you do not believe what you affirm, but imagine you are conciliating your Benin deity by pretending to believe it.'

This correspondent's next (and last) communication was of a very unfriendly character. It reminded one of the letter written by the Ettrick Shepherd after his quarrel with Walter Scott, beginning 'D——d Sir.'

To one who has the experience of a lifetime to look back upon, in which he cannot but have observed how much less important is belief in this and that particular dogma than behaviour, these denunciations seem strange indeed, and what is very remarkable about them is that the vehemence of these good people generally varies inversely with the size of their sect. The fewer, that is, are the professors of a creed, the more positively certain they are of having solved the secrets of the future; however well instructed they may be in Doctrine, it is obviously not 'the Doctrine of Chances.'

There seems nothing more desirable to persons in the vale of years than that pure unquestioning faith which is occasionally found in men, and often in women; but

> Who would rush at a benighted man,
> And give him two black eyes for being blind?

It is surely no sin that, with all the will in the world to believe certain statements, we find great difficulty in accepting them; when withdrawn from 'the dust of creeds,' it seems amazing to us that belief should be considered a voluntary act, within the power of every one who wishes to possess it. Does not He to Whom the sick boy's father cried, 'Lord, I believe; help Thou mine unbelief,' understand how we need help in this matter? To some, indeed, belief may be easy; but why should they plume themselves on this fact; to suppose that there is merit in it is in their case to set a premium on mere credulity. Let them leave these retired veterans who entertain the 'larger hope' alone, and not seek to flatter the God of mercy by attributing to Him atrocities, and saying, 'Nevertheless, since it is Thy will, they are justifiable,' as though He were an Eastern despot.

It is not generally known how often those who have made ever so small a mark in the world from which circumstances have withdrawn them are the objects of this unsought solicitude. As to persons of a wider fame, I have known few indeed who have not suffered from it. It has become, in fact, in their case one of the consequences of old age, and therefore in this brief review of it deserves mention.

It is fair to say that it is not distasteful to everybody. I have even been acquainted with some who welcomed it as a proof of the sympathetic interest they have excited in their fellow-creatures; but the majority dislike it; to some of them it renders their very fame a matter of regret—

> And makes it seem more sweet to be
> The little life of bank and brier,
> The bird that pipes his lone desire,
> And dies unheard within his tree.

THE CLOSING OF THE DOORS

THE CLOSING OF THE DOORS

WHEN I was a boy, one of the many things that puzzle boys, and which they are too proud to ask to be explained to them, was what was the meaning of 'muffled drums.' Now I know, for I am growing very deaf. At first I thought it was one of the warnings which are given us before the last notice to quit this life; but when I consulted a great physician upon the matter, and stated that suspicion, he answered with no little warmth, 'Stuff and nonsense, sir! I am your elder by ten years, and don't intend to be either deaf or blind for many a day. What has happened to you is through what I will call, for want of a better term, "nervous exhaustion."' Then he gave me a prescription, and bade me call upon him again a month later (as it is the hospitable nature of physicians to do) and report myself.

I had not gone to him in the first instance

without being very sure that something was wrong with my hearing; the conviction of which, however, had grown upon me by degrees too slow to detect. At the beginning I heard much too well, sounds that not even Fine Ear himself could have heard, unless suffering from the same disorder. First a buzzing, as though a hive of bees had swarmed, not on my head but in it; then a roaring, as if (though I lived inland) my window had looked out on the ocean; then, particularly at night, sudden explosions, as though a powder magazine had burst in my brain. Like the old lady of Banbury Cross, I had music wherever I went, only not of the same harmonious kind. It was more like what villagers term 'rough music,' as though some good people with marrow-bones and cleavers were trying to persuade the bees in my head to swarm elsewhere, and miserably failed in their endeavours. The real noises which I did hear were made the most of, and reverberated as though I had been the nymph Echo before she fell in love with Narcissus. When a railway train went by, for example, its coming and going lasted for me about the same time that a band consumes in playing the whole of the *Turkish Patrol*, and 'accompanied' with a 'movement' the reverse of 'voluntary' of every nerve in my body.

With this fine volume of sound—quite an *édition de luxe* of it—within, it nevertheless dawned upon me, very gradually, that noises without, unless of the railway train dimensions, were growing dull. It was very curious, but doubtless from some caprice of fashion (perhaps the imitation of talk at Court, which is always carried on in whispers) that the people about me had got into a foolish habit of mumbling. I am naturally rather irritable, and I found myself saying 'What?' with great frequency, and with a sharpness which I could very distinctly hear. Of course I laid this defect upon every cause but the right one, especially the weather, though it was as variable as usual; but at last something occurred which put the matter beyond question. A person with a low, soft voice (one of the gifts of the habitual borrower) asked to see me 'for half a moment on business,' and when in answer to his appeal for five pounds (as I thought it) I buttoned up my pocket and said, 'Not a farthing,' he replied, 'Oh, thank you,' in loud and cheerful tones, and walked off very quickly, I felt that I must have somehow misunderstood the man; but it was not till afterward that I discovered that he had come to *pay* me the five pounds, and that I had most generously declined to accept it. It was then that I felt it high time to consult the doctor. His prescription made me no better, and when at the month's end I went to tell him so, he observed, with all the satisfaction derived from a correct diagnosis, that he had not much expected it would. 'Doctors, in fact, can do nothing for you, my friend,' he continued cheerily. He was of the old Abercrombie school, and a very honest fellow. 'Yours is one of the ailments of which there is little to be said, but "we must grin and bear it."' I thought for the moment of saying, 'But it is you who are grinning, and it is I who am bearing it,' but put the temptation from me. 'Is it any good my going to an aurist?' I inquired instead. 'Oh yes,' he said; then added, with his dry smile, ' to the aurist.'

There are perhaps more stories told against

aurists than against the members of any other profession—and very unfairly. The hearing is a thing very difficult to get at (as I am in a position to corroborate), and cannot be laid on like gas or water, because you can't get the street up to do it. Through the very nature of things aurists must very often fail in effecting a cure, and those they do not benefit are of course dissatisfied with them; moreover it is whispered (and there was a time when I could hear whispers) that deaf people are generally ill-tempered. When I told my friends I was going to consult an aurist, they made themselves very merry about it, and, doubtless that I might join in the joke, roared out to me some capital anecdotes about them, culled from old sources, but new to me. One of them, as a very young man, had gone to an aurist, and this was his experience: The gentleman had held a watch like a golden turnip within a yard or two of his ear. 'Can you hear it tick, my boy?' he inquired loudly. 'No, sir.' 'Can you hear it now?' bringing it nearer. 'No, sir.' 'Can you hear it *now*?' bringing it still nearer. 'Yes, sir.' 'Very good'; then added very loudly indeed, 'My fee is a guinea.' Another had taken his nephew to another auricular professor. He had looked at the lad's ears and said, 'Call again on Tuesday'—and taken his guinea. On Tuesday he made another examination and said, 'Let me see him on Thursday'—and taken it again. On Thursday he blew into the boy's ears and said, 'I think that will do.' When the uncle brought out his guinea as before, the aurist said, 'No, sir, a guinea for a consultation, but for an operation two guineas.'

This was not encouraging, but I went to my aurist nevertheless, and have never repented of it. He examined me very carefully, made certain experiments, and then told me there was nothing amiss with my ears whatever. 'What is the matter with you is nervous deafness. Something has occurred to shock or depress you.' He was quite right. 'I will give you a prescription, but it can do you little good. What you want is fresh air and a constant supply of good news.' He told me honestly what I was to expect, and also what I was still to hope for.

Since then I have been getting gradually worse—so gradually that (as Byron sings of the first day of death) I have sometimes fancied there was a doubt about it; but alas! there is no doubt. In the beginning it made me very irritable; when I could hear only half of what my friends said, [I used to say to myself, 'I think it must be the worst half.' It is always understood that the deaf are more impatient of their calamity, and less agreeable to their fellow-creatures, than the blind. My aurist, who has studied the subject, explains to me the reason of this. The world sees the deaf man at his worst, slow to understand and struggling with his infirmity; and the blind man at his best, partaking of one of the principal pleasures left to him—conversation.

And this brings me to the topic which was what I chiefly had in my mind when I began this little paper. For it is that very pleasure of conversation (to be called such, for all talk that is not 'give and take,' whatever Dr. Johnson may have thought to the contrary, is unworthy of the name) that I have lost for ever; which being so, I can write of it, as few others can, without passion or prejudice, as the true biographer writes of a dead man. For the rest of my life all that I shall get of it is scraps, such as kindly guests at table are moved to throw to the dog whose importunity is disagreeable to the rest of the company. If I could get even them whole, as they leave charitable persons' lips, it would be something; but as often as not I catch only a portion of them, make a frantic guess at the remainder, and generally guess wrong. I had many times seen others do the like, and not, I think, without pity for them; it is some comfort to me now to reflect that I have never seen the hollowed hand raised to the ear, and the eager yet helpless look upon the face of the deaf, without being touched by their calamity. Yet some of the 'bad shots' that are made by these poor fellows who have lost their arms of precision are vastly entertaining, too. I remember it being unanimously agreed in a company that a certain person's nature was lymphatic, save by one member of it who was hard of hearing; nor was it any wonder that he contested the point, since he thought the man had been called 'emphatic.' Again, a young lady more remarkable for her airs than her graces, was described as treating everybody 'with *hauteur.*' 'I am astonished at her doing that,' said a deaf man; and well he might have been, for he thought she had been described as 'treating them to porter.' My own first experience of this jumping at conclusions was amusing enough. I was in the hands of my hair-cutter, and asked him in my affable way where he had spent his holiday. 'I have been abroad, sir,' he replied. 'I never go there,' I answered, 'because I speak no language but my own.' 'Oh, but the people all speak English, sir.' 'You mean the waiters,' I scornfully remarked, 'but I like to speak to everybody.' He said nothing, but stared at me, as though I was going mad as well as bald; nor was it surprising, for where he had told me he had spent his holiday was on the Norfolk Broads.

A man who through his infirmity could make such a mistake as that has surely done with conversation, the very cream and essence of which is to take the meaning as it flies, and 'track suggestion to her inmost cell.' In my

D

time (and this is some consolation to me even now, just as to have once seen the sunshine upon the wave of the wheat must be to those who have become blind) I have met many good talkers, and the best of them have always seemed to be those who had the most alertness for the subject in hand. Though nothing can be less like preaching than this kind of talk, it has in this respect the same relation to other kinds as a good extempore discourse has to an equally good read one. An empty head, unlike a dry well, can often pour forth a 'weak, washy, everlasting flow' of speech on any subject at a moment's notice; but to be able to say the right thing, or the good thing, at the right moment, quickly and brightly, and appositely to the matter in hand, is a rare gift indeed. I knew one that had it, who has long 'joined the majority,' the recollection of whom always recurs to me with a certain sense of splendour. He wears to my eyes, not indeed the halo of the saint (though he was far from a sinner, and indeed a divine), but a sort of aureole of brightness. I find myself once more in an atmosphere of wit and graciousness; it is like sitting next to a beautiful woman, with the unusual addition of never getting tired of her. It so happened that the man I am thinking of made some mark in the world, but that was no addition to his attractions; one never thought of who he was, but of what he said. When he was our companion we did not seem to want for anything; life's cup of pleasure was filled to the brim. Of course he had 'the desire to please,' without which a man may have all the wit and wisdom in the world, but can never possess the charm of the true conversationalist. He was also perfectly natural (another attribute absolutely essential), but had a sententious way with him, which in another would have been set down to affectation. I never see a fountain without thinking of him. We had been talking of the choice of a profession, and what a sad spectacle it was to see so many men in callings that were distasteful to them. 'Happy fountains,' he murmured as we passed some, 'when *they* work, they only play.'

It is not unusual to find persons distinguished in other paths of life—nay, even those who are justly recognised as men of genius—very poor talkers. They hive up their sweet thoughts to put them in their books, and have no honey to spare for their companions; or 'touching the stars with their heads,' they are inconvenienced by stooping to us, and like a tall man walking with his little boy, abstain from conversation for that reason. Some of them, on the other hand, talk a good deal, but not well, though I have always thought that description of Goldsmith, 'He wrote like an angel, but talked like Poor Poll,' must have been an exaggerated one; he could never have been so very dull, for even in the deserts of talk in those of whom I am speaking, there is generally an oasis or two which betrays the real greatness within them. It is only that talk is not their *forte*, just as among whist-players it is rarely the ablest in general intelligence who plays the best rubber. There are, of course, exceptions—men who run through every mode of the lyre and are masters of all. Charles Dickens, for example, was not only one of the best readers, letter-writers, speakers, and actors of his time, but also a charming conversationalist. Considering how accustomed he was to take the public into his confidence, and the immense temptations to which he must have been exposed to address himself to the 'gallery,' his talk was singularly natural, and when on the theme of human life, unrivalled in its interest. It is possible, however that he would not have made a favourable impression at a five-o'clock tea-party.

Women, indeed, although they have a great reputation for 'lifting' conversation, are terribly handicaped at it. I have known only three of the gentler sex who could honestly be placed in the first rank of talkers; nor is this to be wondered at. I was once commissioned by a very liberal and honourable firm to write a boy's story. It was not, at that time, in my line, as I confessed to them, but certain persuasive arguments were used, to which I yielded. Unhappily, after I had consented they wrote me a precautionary letter to warn me that love, crime, the stage, reflections upon things in general, the supernatural, and a long category of all the 'properties' which had hitherto formed my poor stock-in-trade must be carefully avoided. Never since the Israelite was requested to make his bricks without straw by his Egyptian master was employee so put to it. I am bound to say that, though amply remunerated, that story did not turn out a literary success. It was a dance—and indeed a 'break-down'—in fetters. I have always felt a great remorse as regards my relations with that admirable firm, but I also dropped a tear or two for myself. Think of *Hamlet* with not only the Prince left out of it, but the ghost! My position on that unhappy occasion seems to me similar to that of woman in conversation. Almost everything that is really interesting is tabooed to her. In the 'best circles' (which, thank Heaven, I rarely enter) she is said to talk politics. I shall now go to my grave without hearing her discourse upon that topic, but it will add no terror to death. Yet, except politics, how limited, as compared with man's view, are the topics of talk open to her. 'Hear the ladies how they walk, pittle pattle, pittle pattle; hear the ladies how they talk, tittle tattle, tittle tattle,' writes a poet, who treated them as infamously in real life as in his verses;

but how are they to help it? Suppose three-fourths of the subjects on which that savage cynic discoursed to his trembling audience in the coffee-house had been denied to *him*, what reputation as a talker would have survived him? I am no such boor, I hope, as not to have felt the charm of woman's wit and gentleness and refinement; but from the very nature of things woman is unable to speak with man with the openness that men use with one another. The most interesting subject in the world, that of human nature, is to a great extent debarred from them, and religion is a matter their reverent natures shrink from discussing. There is a cynical saying that women are not worth looking at after forty, or worth talking to before; but as regards freedom of conversation (a phrase I am not using, I need not say, in its coarser sense), a woman is generally much older than that before she uses it with mankind. Indeed, the most delightful female talkers I have ever known have been old women, who have mixed much with the world, and whose sympathetic nature has attracted the confidence of both sexes. A young man who has the intelligence to understand them and the grace to perceive the compliment they pay him, will prize such talk, and justly, above all others.

The *raconteur* is often described as a conversationalist, which, however, he either may be or may not be. The man who is always saying, 'That reminds me of an anecdote,' and proceeds to tell it, is generally one to be avoided. But a story that is short and well told and *à propos* is always welcome; and though not the salt of conversation, seasons it very agreeably. I have known excellent talkers of this kind, and when they have been good listeners, they were, to use an old-fashioned term, the best of 'company'; but it is a drawback to many of these story-tellers that they are inclined to monologue. Excited by applause, they endeavour to cap their own anecdote (a most unnatural proceeding) by another, perhaps a very inferior one. Indeed, it is quite amazing how often even a well-practised *raconteur* is destitute of the sense of proportion, and does not understand the difference between what is moderately and what is very good. The true conversationalist possesses this sense in perfection. He is as delicate and sagacious in the manner he handles those with whom he is brought into contact, as in his own behaviour. He persuades the diffident, if they are worth hearing, to speak of their own subjects; he dexterously stops the bore; he imperceptibly steers the bark of conversation from the shallow and the rapid, from the froth of small talk, and from the breakers of argument. Yet no one knows that he is the pilot. The gift, no doubt, is born with him, and, like most other natural gifts, can be improved by practice far more than is generally imagined. On the other hand, it can be almost utterly lost through disuse. An Ariel can never, of course, become a Caliban; but I have known more than one bright spirit through dull surroundings, to lower to the common level, till at last it has seemed to 'sympathise with clay.' So far as I am concerned, alas! they might all be clay—or dust.

To some people it may seem a small thing to know that they shall never again hear a bird sing, or even a cuckoo-clock strike; or to lose the conversation of their friends. But to me the reflection is a very sad one. People who, like the old Marquis of Anglesea after Waterloo, have 'one leg in the grave,' can get on very well with a cork or even a wooden one; but it is not so when one's ears are there. I am thankful to say I never was a great playgoer, or I should feel another of the few pleasures left to those of my time of life cut off. If I want to see a play now (and how appropriate, alas, is that word *see* !), I must have a seat next the orchestra, so that my companion is made almost as deaf as myself. Even then, in five cases out of six, when the house is 'convulsed' I cannot for the life of me understand what it is laughing about. People seem to be made to laugh much more easily than they used to be. Some in the same unhappy position as myself insist upon it that it is 'mere buffoonery' that tickles them so, but I am not so sure of that. Heaven knows I do not grudge them their mirth. But it is sad to have to ask my patient, sweet companion what has been said, and while she is telling me, to the great discontent of my neighbour, we lose the next speech and perhaps the thread of the play. A deaf man is always one speech at least behind the rest of the world; and to me, at least, it makes a great difference. Let us hope we get our hearing back, with all other good things we miss, in heaven. By the by, I wonder who has got my hearing? Force of any kind, men of science tell us, is never lost, but must needs go somewhere or other. I hope whosoever has my hearing will have the same opportunities and make as good use of it as I did. What bright and genial utterances, what assurances of love and friendship, what wit and wisdom have entered at those once open doors! I have stored and garnered much of the treasure of talk that has been lavished upon me. I have listened to speech that has been better than 'silver,' and compared with which the silence that has befallen me is far indeed from 'golden'; and now that I shall never hear it more, how inestimable it seems! As the man who has lost his sight pictures with the mental eyes that are still left to him 'the pleasant fields and farms,' the sea with its 'innumerable smile,' and the well-remembered faces of his dear ones, so I conjure up with the same tender sense of loss and melancholy joy the conversation of my friends.

Though depressed myself, however, I have no wish to depress others; I have always been for the smile against the sigh, and do not grudge the world what they may find jocose in my calamity. Unlike the blind, the deaf have ever been a subject of mirth to their fellow-creatures, just as the gout (to those who haven't got it) is a matter of never-failing jest. The latest humorous anecdotes connected with my little drawback have been kindly written out for me by a friend. In a company conversing of the Indian Mutiny, some one said of a rebel who fell into the hands of the British, 'He had me a short shrift.' 'What did that matter,' observed a deaf gentleman contemptuously, 'in so warm a climate?' A gentleman averse to lavishness, and hard of hearing, but not quite so hard, it was whispered, as he sometimes pretended to be, was applied to by a friend for a loan. 'Will you lend me half a sovereign?' 'What?' 'Will you lend me a sovereign?' 'You said just now *half* a sovereign.'

NOW AND THEN IN HOME LIFE

NOW AND THEN IN HOME LIFE

WHEN Scott wrote *Waverley* he took for its second title *'Tis Sixty Years Since*, having in his mind, no doubt, the immense changes that had taken place in social life during that period. Almost the same interval of time has passed since the accession of our gracious Queen, and it has been marked by changes infinitely greater in science, history, and politics, and almost as great in domestic life. Half a century ago, long before agricultural depression had cast its shadow on 'the Land,' families in the country belonging to the upper middle classes had a very good time of it, much better than those of the same rank in the towns. All the men, and some of the women, were centaurs; even the boys had ponies, often chosen from the droves from Wales, which at that time visited our southern counties. To ride well was not then an accomplishment, it was supposed to be a natural gift, and not to like it argued something amiss in the moral sense; if, therefore, intelligent youths preferred literature to hunting, they dissembled their love, which was my own case.

I could stick on a horse with the tenacity of a monkey, but liked it about as little; my one rule of horsemanship was not to be thrown. This was not, unhappily, discovered early, and my friends, who were all equine, used often to give me a mount, and imagine they placed me under an obligation. The mistake almost cost the life of an M.F.H. Somebody had lent me a young horse, for which I thanked him with alien lips, to hunt one day in Wiltshire; as the beast fretted and curveted I heard the lender, riding behind me with a friend, expatiating upon its merits. He would not have lent it to everybody, but that lad (myself) knew what he was about. I did not know, however, what the horse was about, and 'gave him his head,' which I had been warned to do, simply because he took it. In an early part of the run we came to a hedge with a fall on the other side; there was a gap, which of course I took, and got over safely enough, but within one inch or so of the head of the Master of the Hounds, whom I had followed too quickly, and whose horse had fallen with him. The fuss that was made about that business—though surely a pure accident—destroyed, thank Heaven, my reputation as a horseman, and I was much too sagacious to attempt to recover it. From that moment I was looked upon in the domestic circle as one from whom no good was to be expected.

There are much fewer equine families now, from want of money and the introduction of the two-wheeled steed, but years ago horses became less necessary from the facilities for locomotion afforded by the railways. These have begotten more changes, moral, material, and social, than all other causes put together. In my youth every household in the country of the least pretension had some wheeled conveyance; though many of them were of an unambitious character. I remember one owned by a magistrate and deputy-lieutenant of his county, which, from its unparalleled and indefinite nature, was called 'The Thing.' It was like a postchaise (then going out of fashion), with curtains instead of a window, which did not afford much protection in the storms and breezes of the Berkshire downs. Moreover, it must have been ill put together, for the coachman drove home one day with only half the vehicle, leaving his master and mistress on the Roman Ridgeway, exposed to the elements.

Those were years of plenty, but not as yet of luxury. Girls did not disdain to ride in 'skirts'; smoking in most country houses was not allowed, and young gentlemen of birth and position had to take their pipes to the saddle-room. Champagne was rarely seen even at the best tables; the story of the chaplain who, when he saw the tall glasses, used to change his ordinary grace for a more florid one, was, perhaps, founded on fact, for the treat was exceptional; and the wine very likely was not iced. Folks were contented with simple amusements, but pursued them with great zeal and an utter disregard for comfort. They would drive ten miles to a dinner-party and fifteen to a county ball; at home they would play round games for 'fish at sixpence a dozen,' and yet manage to quarrel over them; their highest form of diversion was private theatricals. When these occurred, guests would go through fire and water—indeed often did go through water—in order to be present. The village my people lived in was in a valley high up among the downs, and in winter we were generally imprisoned for a week or two, the deep roads running down to us on all sides being choked with snow, which lay in deep and dangerous drifts. The treeless fields could not be discerned from one another, but this did not stop us from venturing over them when a play was to be seen. I remember a party of a dozen, half of them ladies, packing into a wagon drawn by six dray horses, and traversing that wintry waste, like the exiles of Siberia, but in much better spirits. Every now and then one of the drivers—there were three of them, off and on—would express his fear that we were 'getting nigh a road,' when there would be discussion and digression. We arrived somehow at our journey's end, and what was more wonderful, got home again, and nobody thought anything of the adventure.

The country gentry drank much more than they do now, port and sherry rather than claret. The after-dinner coffee and cigars, which have done more to put an end to drunkenness among the upper classes than all our teachers and preachers, were unknown; yet the habit of heavy drinking was already dying away. There was more rheumatism (from exposure and carelessness about health) than at present, and notwithstanding the out-of-door life, more gout; but that ingenious combination of those diseases of which 'kindly nature' now gives us so many examples, and the doctors—'giving a name to what they cannot cure'—call *rheumatoid arthritis*, was much more rare. Many more 'gentlemen sportsmen' were brought home on hurdles with broken necks; but, on the whole, paterfamilias lived quite as long as he does now without the slightest attention to sanitation. When he expired, it was with no assistance from any specialist from London; if one had been sent for, indeed, he could hardly have arrived in time, unless, like Charles II., the patient took an unconscionable time in dying.

The profession that has prospered most (though, of course, it is terribly overstocked) in these days is that of the physician. Not only do paterfamilias and his wife, when anything serious is amiss with them, come up to town for 'an opinion,' but also their children; notwithstanding the hard times, the doubling of the guinea for a first visit—a financial revolution accomplished with such suddenness and secrecy that one hardly heard of it till it was a success—does not seem to have deterred them in the least. A vast deal more money is now spent in the pursuit of health than of old. Rare is the family of which some member or branch of it has not been recommended to leave England for Davos Platz or the Riviera, for Colorado or Algiers, for cold countries or hot ones, and all for the same complaint. The foreign God's-acres are more crowded in consequence, but our doctors thus relieve themselves from grave responsibilities. Separations between parents and children, which when the former are far gone in years is a sort of premature death, are much more common. The want of occupation at home, and the necessity for providing for themselves, causes our sons to migrate to distant lands far more than of old; while, on the other hand, improved postal communication and the telegraphs keep them within touch of one another. Among the poor, the fate of their sons on service is no longer a matter ignored by the military authorities; the parents are not left in doubt as to whether Tom or Dick is alive or dead. In old times the widow who inquired at the 'office' after her soldier boy was treated with scant tenderness. 'Tom Atkins, do you say? Dead. Our fee is a shilling. You mustn't cry here; cry in the yard.' Now his end is recorded by the wire, and transmitted to her, as though he had a commission.

Our juveniles have become of much more consequence every way; novels are written to show their immense influence in the world; it seems quite strange that their admittance to Parliament, like that of women, has not been made a 'platform.' They are now the dominant race, but I can remember when it was quite otherwise. They were pitchforked into schools (and sometimes out of them) without much care or scruple; their complaints were not listened to, though they had often good cause to make them; and authority over them of a despotic kind was often delegated to unfit persons. I remember one striking instance of this. Our house in the country had been let to a family, the head of which was on service in India, and I was asked to stay there for a week; the two boys who were to be my playmates were older than myself, indeed almost grown up, fourteen or fifteen; their mother was a lady of some fashion, who took little interest in her children, and everything, even in the way of punishment, was deputed to a virago of a nurse, very bony and strong, whose appearance reminded me of Mother Brownrigg, just then very popular in wax exhibitions. On the first evening, at tea-time, some difference of opinion arose between this person and the boys, whereupon she opened a cupboard, produced from it a stick, much thicker than any cane, and proceeded to beat both her young masters with passionate energy. It was quite a humiliation to see those wretched boys flying about the room, and receiving, without a word of remonstrance or attempt at resistance, her pitiless blows. What heightened the shame of it was that they were by no means cowed or spiritless in their ordinary behaviour, but submitted to this ignominious chastisement as a matter of course.

Such Spartan discipline as this was no doubt exceptional, but children were kept in strict subjection. We hear mothers nowadays say of some *enfant terrible*, 'The dear boy is never spoilt, but only indulged'; but in those times there was very little even of indulgence. Strange to say, this harshness did not weaken the feeling of kinship; indeed, the bond of blood was much stronger than it is now. Our circle of acquaintance has vastly increased with the facilities of locomotion; we are no longer dependent on our relatives for society, and often meet with other people who are more to our taste. This is seen in the gradual falling off of family gatherings on domestic anniversaries or at Christmas-time. Through the influence of Dickens's works there was a temporary resuscitation of them, but it is now well understood that the best chance of the preservation of

John's brotherly affection for Harriet, and for Henrietta's love for dear Tom, is that they should meet as seldom as possible.

The difficulty of 'placing' our boys in any position where they can maintain themselves is far worse than it used to be, but they have a greater independence of manner. In this respect our girls are not behind them. They are not, perhaps, less modest than their grandmothers, who never ventured to speak of their male acquaintances as 'men,' but always as 'gentlemen,' but their behaviour with them is certainly more familiar, a habit, I observe, which is not, however, permanently attractive even with the objects of their favour.

We are much more gregarious than we used to be, but prefer to choose our own company. A man of distinction, by no means a 'diner-out,' in a fashionable sense, once assured me that he had never dined alone (except when he was ill) for the last thirty years; a curious fact enough when one thinks of the many old fellows who dine at our clubs every day with no companion opposite to them but a book or a newspaper. Among the upper classes it is the clubs which have done most to destroy the family bond, and not only in the way of marriage. Club friends and family friends are kept quite distinct, and we often see more of the former than the latter. Sixty years since only a few men, even of good position, belonged to a club. It is now the first ambition of our sons, when they have attained what are humorously termed 'years of discretion,' to join one of these establishments.

Though in almost every respect we have become more luxurious, there is much less pretence than there used to be. Young men and women of the upper classes did not of old frequent the theatres as they do now, but when they did go they sat in the stalls; it is true these were then only half the price they have reached of late years, but it was not the comparative cheapness that caused them to be patronised; the differences of social position were more insisted upon. Nowadays the same classes go to the dress circle, or upper boxes, though not to the pit, which half a century ago had lost its once proud position in the eyes of playgoers. Girls of good family now affect the 'bike' and the ''bus,' and to travel in a first-class railway carriage has become quite a distinction in circles which were wont to use no other. In the club smoking-room the humble briar-root is as much patronised as the Havana cigar; there is hardly any dandyism in the way of apparel; 'ducks,' once such popular wear, are as extinct as the dodo, but 'flannels' are fast taking their place.

These improvements do not, one regrets to say, arise from any admiration of economy in our young people, but rather from the wish to get as much pleasure out of life with the means at their disposal as possible, but, on the whole, they are dictated by common-sense. In comparing our domestic life with that of our forefathers, I am inclined to think, notwithstanding the anti-everythingarians and faddists who infest modern society, that this is the virtue on which we have most right to plume ourselves. Nowhere has it made itself more felt than in religious matters. I can remember when the heads of families, as a general rule, thought it their duty to lay a burthen on the conscience of their offspring heavier than they could bear, in teaching them that the Creator had doomed a large proportion of His creatures to suffer in the next world eternal tortures in a lake of fire. It was nothing less than the worship of the devil, against which, of course, every instinct of humanity in the children, as they grew up, revolted in dismay. This was the cause of many sharp opinions and bitter conflicts, which sometimes ended in the exile of the youthful martyr, and the dear-bought victory of his misguided parents. If such a hateful creed still here and there exists, it can no longer be enforced by its possessor; 'the common-sense of most' is too strong for him; so far as its powers for evil are concerned, it is 'an extinct Satan'; but for years it 'shook the pillars of domestic peace.'

An error of another kind which flourished sixty years since among the upper classes, but is now everywhere discouraged, was the contempt they had for commerce. Except in the case of bankers (whom they dared not despise) they looked down on everybody who derived his income from this source. The young gentlemen were quite as great fools as their fathers in this respect, and thought themselves heroic in preferring a profession with probable penury to an assured competence with their hands soiled by trade. This absurd prejudice is now as much ridiculed by our gilt youth as by any other class. One of them lately became engaged to the ward of a gentleman of the old school, who thought it necessary to apologise for a certain blot on her scutcheon. 'I have to confess, my dear sir, that her family have been quite recently connected with trade.' 'I am sorry——' began the young man gravely. 'So am I,' put in the old fellow, a little testily, for it did not please him that his prejudice should be reciprocated, 'but it can't be helped.' 'I was about to say,' continued the young man, 'I am sorry that you should have thought me such a stupendous ass as to care twopence about it.'

ON CONVERSATION

ON CONVERSATION

THE art of conversation has suffered in England from the example of its most famous professor. Dr. Johnson understood it theoretically, but even so only to a limited extent. He was supposed to form his view of it in accordance with the rule of Bacon.

In all kinds of speech, whether pleasant, grave, severe, or ordinary, it is convenient to speak leisurely, and rather drawlingly than hastily, because hasty speech confounds the memory, and oftentimes, besides the unseemliness, drives a man either to stammering, or nonplus, or harping on that which should follow; whereas a slow speech conformeth the memory, addeth a conceit of wisdom to the hearers, besides a seemliness of speech and countenance.

This does not strike one as a model for him who would be either brilliant or agreeable, and excludes naturalness, which is one of the greatest charms of conversation.

That Johnson did not slavishly follow Bacon's

precept is very certain. So far from being 'leisurely,' he jumped down the throats of all who disagreed with him. 'You may be good-natured, sir,' said Boswell, with unusual spirit, 'but you are not good-humoured' (which the Doctor had just plumed himself on being). 'I believe you would pardon your opponents if they had time to deprecate your vengeance; but punishment follows so quick after sentence that they cannot escape.' The idea of his ever being at a nonplus is ridiculous indeed, though he was sometimes at a loss for a repartee from sheer indignation. The rights of his little passage-of-arms with Adam Smith are much disputed. That he remarked: 'You are a liar,' seems tolerably certain, but whether the other philosopher did retort in the quite unprintable and by no means pertinent words that are attributed to him is doubtful. At all events, the whole affair was not a good example of polite conversation. Johnson's great mistake was in confounding it with monologue. 'We had good talk this evening,' he said on one occasion, when returning from a party where scarcely any one had been able to get a word in edgeways except himself. If he had said: '*I* had good talk,' the observation would have been faultless, but of conversation such as he sincerely believed had taken place there had been none. He could define it of course as he could everything else, and sometimes affected to despise it. When Boswell asked him, in his importunate fashion, what was the use of meeting people at dinner, where no one ever said anything worth remembering, 'Why, to eat and drink together,' replied the Doctor, 'and to promote kindness; and, sir, this is better done when there is no solid conversation; for when there is, people differ in opinion and get into bad humour, or some of the company are left out and feel themselves uneasy; it was for this reason that Sir Robert Walpole said he always talked indecencies at his own table, because in them all could join.' It is certain that this was the kind of conversation most in vogue with our ancestors, and in 'the good old times,' such as the days of chivalry, there was probably little else.

Later on, and even to some extent to-day, the essence of good conversation was thought to be contest. Even that graceful-minded and sweet-tempered writer, Robert Louis Stevenson, falls into the error when discoursing on this subject. With Johnson, opposition was the very salt of life, and his best sayings were evoked by it. When ill one day and unable to exert himself, on Burke's name being mentioned, he suddenly exclaimed: 'That fellow calls forth all my powers. Were I to see Burke now it would kill me.'

Antagonism of all kinds is, however, inimical to social enjoyment, and even argument should be employed but sparingly. The object of good conversation is not to convince—we are not pleading at the Bar, or preaching in the Pulpit—but to exchange ideas, expressed in the most attractive form, to ameliorate, to interest, or to amuse. It is a mistake to suppose that a change of society is necessary for its enjoyment. When friends are found to our mind, we do not tire of their talk. It is not likely, though it is quite possible, that a stranger may be an acquisition, and a company of intelligent persons who meet one another are independent of recruits.

Goldsmith, who never wrote a foolish thing and seldom said a wise one, thought differently; he expressed a wish for some additional members to be added to the Literary Club. 'For there can be now,' he said, 'nothing new among us; we have travelled over one another's minds'; to which Johnson calmly but confidently observed: 'Sir, you have not travelled over *my* mind, I promise you.' The Doctor, of course, was so exceptionally gifted that it was a treat to listen to him, if a man were content to deprive himself of the right of reply; but he had no notion of the 'give and take,' without which there is no social intercourse.

A good talker should be a good listener, though also capable of cutting short a bore; he should be appreciative of the remarks of others, and never influenced by that vulgar rivalry that causes some men to strive for the mastery in anecdote—the 'capping' of stories, as old writers term it. Anecdotes, however apt and witty, are, after all, a form of monologue, and should be used with discretion. Even the best *raconteurs* are tempted to draw too largely upon their deposit accounts; a certain intoxication seems to seize those not in the very first rank when they have made a success or two in this line, and I have known one with a great reputation who could never be trusted after a capital story not to wipe out the remembrance of it by a dull one. He really did not seem to know what was good and what was indifferent; he had a large quantity of the commodity (anecdote) on his hands, and must needs get rid of it at any cost to his reputation. A high-class but still detestable talk-stopper is the man of rounded periods. Everybody knows how he is going to finish his sentences, but he will do it his own way, and it is a long way round. One is inclined to say to him what Scrooge so pathetically observed to his partner's ghost, 'Don't be flowery, my friend, don't be flowery.'

These are by no means the greatest obstructionists in the way of conversation. Some persons might almost be called professional talk-stoppers. They delight in questioning the truth of a good story, or in picking some hole in it, to prove that it had a better reception than it deserved. They lay their finger on some trivial inaccuracy in a date or a name; they bring no provender to the intellectual picnic; their sole contribution to it is a senseless depreciation, which they conscientiously believe adds to the agreeableness of the evening. I wish no fellow-creature dead, but I do think this class of person should be relegated to some other sphere of usefulness, where (like Miss Snevellicci's papa) he would be appreciated. It is all very well to say, 'Let us have no cliques,' but some precaution must be taken to keep persons of this sort out of any society which has a claim to consider itself agreeable.

In old days a very innocent but still very effectual talk-stopper was the Child. Parents used to bring their terrible infants into grown-up company, even of an intelligent kind. It was an outrage of that description which caused Charles Lamb to propose the health of Herod, King of the Jews. In scarcely a less degree (though one hesitates to acknowledge it) the presence of the Young Person of either sex is to be deprecated.

Some persons have the rudeness to go further, and assert that in the presence of the gentler sex conversation, not so much of an intellectual but of a natural or dramatic, and especially of a humorous kind, can seldom be carried on. It has been said, indeed, that a bright and clever woman 'lifts the conversation' at dinner-parties, but what sort of conversation do we generally find at dinner-parties? And what must the conversation be that requires 'lifting'? It is quite true that the talk of a polished and educated woman, of mature years and a liberal mind, is one of the most delightful of intellectual pleasures—it has well been called a liberal education; but how rare such women are! And how terribly even *they* are handicaped! They can talk of literature, of politics, and even of religion, though in the last case seldom with any freedom; but speculations on 'fate, free will, foreknowledge absolute,' the subjects of the best kind of conversation, are not to their taste, while from the discussion of some of the most interesting topics connected with human nature they are of necessity debarred. A better and wiser adviser of a young man in social matters is not to be found than in some ancient lady of wealth and position, whose very voice has persuasion in it, and who speaks from the fulness of her own knowledge. 'I am an old woman, you know. Tell me your trouble.' But that is only a duet, though one of exquisite sympathy; the talk of two. As a rule women's talk, like that of the aristocracy, is almost always personal.

The flippancies and cynicism of the smoking-room are very naturally in ill odour; yet the brightest conversations within my own somewhat extensive experience have been held under the benign influence of tobacco. It nourishes quiet thought and does away with ill-humour; smokers do not talk unless they have something to say, and are careful to say it not at too great length, or their pipe would go out. Thus anecdote is restrained within proper limits, and monologue is rendered impossible.

It is rather invidious to pronounce which profession produces the best conversationalists, and such a judgment must be open to many exceptions; it can be at most but a general impression; but on the whole—there is nothing like leather—I think men of letters are the best talkers. It is true they are sometimes the worst from a negative point of view, since some of them cannot talk at all. The sole channel of their intelligence is their pen. But the higher class of literary men have generally something interesting to say, because they are students of human nature, and adapt their experiences of it to their company. They never talk of their own books, nor very much even of literature. One of the many gifts of Charles Dickens was that of public speaking; but his conversation with his intimates was still more delightful; not at all witty, but intensely humorous, though combined with great earnestness, however slight might be the subject. He disliked general society, chiefly, I think, from the fear that some foolish person would compliment him to his face, a stroke of vulgarity that requires a master of fence indeed to parry.

Lever was a *raconteur* of the first sparkle, but after an hour or two one had enough of him. The best conversationalist I ever knew (that is, among the departed) was a man of letters, W. G. Clark; he was one of the editors of the *Cambridge Shakespeare*, and the author of *Summer Months in Spain*, but had a higher reputation as a classical scholar. He 'wore his weight of learning like a flower,' which is by no means usually the case with learned persons: they have no 'buttonhole' themselves, but they buttonhole other people, and their perception of humour is generally confined to a false quantity. I can never understand why this error should be so mirth-provoking in a dead language, and so devoid of amusement in a living one.

Small literary folks are seldom good company, they talk literature too much; and though it is the best 'shop' to talk about, 'shop' is always better left alone. Observe how a soldier with a record of distinguished service avoids it; from a certain fine sense of modesty no less than good taste. He is as difficult to draw as a badger, but when drawn gives excellent sport. I am not one of those literary persons who seem to take a pleasure (for it is always affected) in contrasting to his disparagement Captain Pen with Captain Sword (for it is something, as now happens, 'to have at one's back a million men'); but I must admit that there are few kinds of talk so attractive as that of the unwilling warrior making light of experiences which, if they had happened to me, I feel with a secret blush, would have formed a more constant topic of conversation.

The talk of barristers is often very clever, but too inclined to be shoppy; they remind one of public school men, who, after they have ceased to be boys for half a century, will still retail the reminiscences of that far-back time to one another, without much consideration for that portion of the company who have neither been at Eton nor Harrow. The men of the gown are bright enough, but even when good-natured are too apt to affect cynicism, which destroys at one blow both geniality and naturalness.

'The lower branch of the profession' are generally silent and severe (wherefore, I know not, and Heaven forbid that I should draw the secret from its 'dread abode'), but now and then we get an admirable specimen from this collection. There is nothing like your 'family lawyer' as a receptacle of secrets, matters of real human interest, and sometimes he will open a closet without divulging its whereabouts, and show you a skeleton.

I had once a friend who had no rival as an exhibitor of this description—the happiest mixture of grave and gay conceivable, and who possessed quite an anatomical museum. Some of the heads of families he had to deal with deserved a fuller portraiture at the hands of the dramatist or the novelist, but as sketches they were faultless. I remember one of them, and wish I could reproduce the touches which gave to the original picture its life and likeness. The man was a wealthy and still young north-country squire, selfish and self-indulgent; childless, which was fortunate, for he was very unfit to play a father's part; and suddenly widowed. It was to the funeral of the wife that my friend was professionally invited. It had not been a happy marriage. The man was gloomy, not because of his bereavement, but because of the solemnity and seriousness it entailed. He would have gone away, if he had dared, and left her relations to bury her; he did not like them, and swore he would not be shut up in a carriage with any one of them—

he would ride alone. 'No,' said my friend, who had great influence over him (as indeed he had over most people which whom he was brought into contact), 'you must not do that.' There were good reasons why he should not have gone alone. 'If you will not go with your relatives you must go with the clergyman.' 'The clergyman! Well, if I must, I must, but it will quite spoil my day.'

Another funeral story, but against himself, he told with inimitable humour. I say 'told,' not 'used to tell,' for I never heard him repeat the same experience. The measures he took with his clients were represented as so successful that I requested him on one occasion to tell me one of his failures. For one instant he looked confused, but immediately resumed his serenity.

Well, I have been young like everybody else. When junior partner in my firm, I went down to the funeral of a client, very rich but not respected. He had no relatives and no friends, but there were a great many mourning-coaches. It was winter, and the burial-place was five miles from the Hall. I was in the last coach with the doctor, a young man like myself. We went at a good pace over the snow, and the whole proceeding was tedious and disagreeable. 'Do you think,' said the doctor, 'there would be any harm in our having a cigar?' Of course it was wrong, and very unprofessional in both of us, but we lit up. It was a great relief, and, as we flattered ourselves, unaccompanied by danger. Presently, however, the whole line—about five-and-twenty carriages—came to a dead stop. The undertaker and one of his men ran wildly to our window. 'Gentlemen, your carriage is on fire!' It cost us a couple of sovereigns, but we escaped detection.

Taking them all round, I had rather talk with a strange doctor than a stranger of any other profession. They have generally seen a great deal of human nature, and if they have only seen a little of it, it is worth hearing about. They never talk about Art, at all events. I confess I am rather afraid of travellers, unless they are commercial travellers. They are too full of information, and are too often anxious to impart it. Sometimes it is not even true. Frederic Locker used to tell of how an unscrupulous traveller narrating his adventures among the Red Indians was cleverly stopped by Lord Barrymore. 'Did you ever see anything of the Chick-Chows?' 'Oh! a good deal,' aid Sir Arthur, 'a very cruel tribe, the Chick-Chows.' 'And the Cherry-Chows, eh?' 'Oh, very much among the Cherry-Chows,' continued Sir Arthur; 'the Cherry-Chows were singularly kind to my fellows.' 'And pray, Sir Arthur, did you see much of the Tol-de-roddy-bow-wows?'

This was too much for even Sir Arthur. He was rather put out, but the company was relieved. Nevertheless, there *are* modest travellers. I had once a great friend who had travelled all round the world. When almost on his deathbed, he spoke to me on the subject for the first time, with humorous pathos. 'My dear fellow, you will do me the justice, when I am gone, to say that I never told you one word about it.' But he was an noble exception.

As to the clergy, they are a good deal weighted as regards conversation. Coleridge once observed that Nature was the Devil in a strait-waistcoat. Clergymen are Angels similarly attired. There are, and have been, however, great exceptions: Sydney Smith, for example, whom no layman, except perhaps Douglas Jerrold, has ever excelled for brightness, and none have equalled for geniality. How much conversation has to do with manners may be gathered from the biographies of witty persons. How dull they are!

Folks talk of 'the art of conversation,' and of course there are some rules which need to be observed by all who would excel in it: to be brief, without curtness; to avoid any 'talking to the gallery' (but indeed in the sort of company I have in my mind there is no gallery); to give and take. But the fact is, conversation is a gift of nature; when artificial, it is never really good. The disposition must be genial, the wit ready and keen, but of the kind that 'never carries a heart-stain away on its blade'; the humour abundant, but always arising from the situation; not pumped up, but a natural flow; there must be a quick sympathy, and, above all, the desire to please.

ON TAKING OFFENCE

ON TAKING OFFENCE

IN a social point of view, when you have said that a man is an offensive fellow, you have said the worst of him, or that can be said. He may be in his private capacity a forger or, as is much more likely, a murderer; but, so far as his attitude to society is concerned, the revelation of that circumstance would put him in no worse position; on the contrary, while his character would in nowise be deteriorated, it would invest him with a certain dramatic interest, and, even if the worst came to the worst, it would be very pleasant to see him hanged.

Every one knows an offensive fellow at the first glance: he can no more conceal his disposition than the skunk can deodorise himself; in nine cases out of ten indeed it is evident in his face, the expression of which, like a tavern-sign, unfortunately frank, informs us that sour wine is sold within; but if not, he has only to open his mouth and out flies the truth about him; for this hateful creature always prefers to say a disagreeable thing to you instead of an agreeable one, and cannot hold his tongue.

To this class belong bullies and backbiters, in whose favour no one has a word to say, and at whose decease the very ingrates move their tardy lips in thankfulness. Under these circumstances it seems strange that the adjective 'inoffensive' should not carry more praise with it; whereas when applied to one's fellow-creatures it has rather a contemptuous significance. The term 'good-natured' is not very eulogistic; as the poet most familiar to my boyhood rather abruptly observes,

> Oh! what is mere Good-nature but a Fool?

but 'Inoffensiveness,' if personified and described in song, would probably come off even worse. The explanation of this is, no doubt, that every one, it is felt, should have what is called 'a kick in him'; the capability, not indeed of giving offence, but, if it is offered to us, of giving it back again. There are degrees between the hornet and the humble-bee, and every one should have a sting in his tail, ready for use on occasion.

I cannot help thinking, however, that there is another reason for the depreciation of inoffensive folk. They have such a want of self-assertion that they never give the least ground for quarrel. And though it is only the morose and evil-disposed who like a grudge, there are a good many of us who like a grievance. To take offence where no offence is meant, and where they *know* none is meant, is also a great joy to some natures; and these naturally resent a state of things wherein, even by the utmost ingenuity, the intention of hurting their feelings cannot be imputed.

To the grievance-monger there is nothing so objectionable as an explanation. It is putting out the fire beside which he nurses his wrath and keeps it warm. In the atmosphere of his discontent, his wrong has assumed gigantic proportions, and it is very disagreeable to see it melt away in the wholesome air of common-sense. When we see a play on the stage built up on some misunderstanding which three words would dissipate, we exclaim 'How absurd! How unnatural!' but these people weave a life-drama for themselves out of these very materials, and take their pleasure in a maze of feelings warranted of their own manufacture. They are always on the look-out for slights; a depreciatory observation, a glance which can be construed to imply contempt, is at once furnished with a personal application, and provides them with their desideratum; even silence has been known to furnish it. The 'Hurt' family, to which they belong, has many branches, but the type is the same throughout. If fortune, so far from being 'outrageous,' has neither strings nor arrows, there are at least nettles to be found, and they proceed to divest themselves of their last garment and roll in them. Nothing is more amusing than to see these people unexpectedly confronted with a real grievance: some elephantine person who is accustomed to put his foot down, and is not particular where he puts it. They are like boys who, 'ranging the woods to start a hare,' come on a sudden upon a fierce old bear, who 'lies amid bones and blood.' The homœopathic remedy which the schoolmaster applies to whining children—the 'giving them something to cry for'—is most efficacious. It must be said, however, for this class of persons, that they are ready enough to accept an apology; which indeed does them no harm, since they can discover a new cause of offence within the next five minutes.

A much more contemptible variety is to be found in those who refuse to be conciliated; who will not take those words, alike gentle and simple, 'I am sorry,' in the sense in which they are uttered. This generally arises from petty egotism; the sense of quarrel seems to invest them with a certain importance, which they have no other means of attaining; they prefer to be unreasonable, and therefore to some extent extraordinary, rather than to return to their original position of insignificance.

There is still a worse class, who seek in discord a channel for their evil temper, which is always at the flood. They have a bad word for everybody, but a particularly bad one (which is also generally a falsehood) for the object of their private rancour. The Corsican, ignorant, idle, and venomous, is the head of this charming family. The art of taking offence in his case is not only carried to the most delicate perfection, but is hereditary.

Nevertheless, a certain King of Scotland must needs be placed at the head of this profession, inasmuch as he took offence by proxy. Perceiving one of his courtiers to have lost an eye, he inquired the reason. 'It was put out by accident by a fencing-master,' was the reply.

'And is that man alive?' inquired his majesty significantly.

Whereupon the courtier, recalled to a sense of what was due to himself as a nobleman and a Christian, at once went and murdered the innocent offender.

It must be remembered in charity that accidents of birth and blood, or even family misfortunes, make people quick to take offence. When one's father has been hanged, an allusion to a rope, even by one who has never heard of the deplorable occurrence, is apt to grate on the ear. A personal blemish or deformity will, in a sensitive nature, have the same unfortunate effect. One of the kindest men I ever knew, and certainly the very last to give offence to any human being, was once a victim to this circumstance. When a boy, he was on the Chain Pier at Brighton with his mother, a lady also of exceptionally gentle nature, when an umbrella blown inside out chanced to excite their mirth. A woman sitting next to them at once arose and favoured them with this amazing speech, 'An ill-bred woman, and a worse taught child!' They then perceived for the first time that she had what is called a port-wine stain on her cheek, to which, I suppose, as in the case of Byron and his club foot, this poor lady imagined that every one was directing their attention. An apology was out of the question; but I am very sure that the child and his parent suffered far more than the injured party.

Misunderstandings which might easily be rectified are often followed, in the mean time, by actions which admit of no remedy. In a country town, where I once lived as a boy, the virulence with which two men hated one another was quite a proverb. Mr. A. and Dr. B. had once been intimate friends, and though one was a Tory and the other a Radical, had agreed to differ: they could even afford to rally one another upon the vehemence of their respective opinions.

'For all your high and dry principles,' said B., when the news came of Queen Caroline's acquittal, 'you will have to illuminate your house to-night.'

'There shall not be a candle,' returned A. defiantly.

The next morning Dr. B. met his friend, and congratulated him, since the violence of the mob had been very great, that he had thought better of his resolution, and taken the prudent course of lighting up his house.

'I did nothing of the kind,' said A.

'Then I don't know what you call lighting up; it was so well done, however, that I hear the mob gave you three cheers.'

'That is false,' replied A. excitedly, and—not to go into painful details—a blow was given and returned.

The fact was that A. had gone out to dinner,

and his wife, in spite of his injunctions, and preferring unbroken windows to principles intact, had lit up the house, without his knowledge. A. and B. went to their graves without exchanging another word with each other.

After all, those who speak with the deliberate intention of giving offence—the 'Roughs' of polite society—are not numerous. Some women will, however, 'say things' to persons of their own sex which to our ears sound outrageous, and would not be tolerated for a moment by men from a man. The reason of this is that, though women have a reputation for badinage (as they have, less deservedly, for 'tact'), they shrink from all retort, save 'the retort courteous.' They cannot reply when a disagreeable thing is said, 'Well, upon my word, you're a nice, agreeable, ladylike person, *you* are'; or even, 'Do you really think that remark of yours exhibits the desire, so insisted on by moralists, to increase the happiness of the human family?' There are many ways of stopping the mouth of a disagreeable male, besides putting your fist in it, which are denied to the gentler sex.

The consciousness of this—of there being no remedy in case of the thing going too far—is perhaps the reason why women do not rally one another, as men do; with the latter a certain good-humoured chaff, among old friends, is as the bread of life to social intercourse: women chaff the other sex, but not their own. They say 'our tempers will not stand it; we are less good-natured to one another than you are'; but the real cause is, I believe, as I have stated it.

He who has the wish to please need never fear giving offence; those who take it under such circumstances mistake egotism for self-respect, moroseness for dignity, and are among the chief obstructives to human enjoyment.

TAKING THE WATERS

TAKING THE WATERS

AUTUMN is the season in which your chronic invalids, the victims chiefly of *rheumatoid arthritis*, that new and euphonious term for the old rheumatic gout of our forefathers, proceed to take the waters either abroad or at home, and very diverse accounts they give of them. One swears by them, and another swears at them. In this country they are mostly situated in the North, and Scotchmen protest that there is no place like Glenhoulakin (as nearly as I can spell it), where the waters bubble up at exactly the right temperature to make toddy. To the Southerners these places seem 'a little cold for the time of year,' and the water is by no means all subterranean, but comes down from the grey clouds in sheets. Still, what does that signify if you arrive like a corkscrew (from the *rheumatoid arthritis*) and go away like a ramrod, cured? This beneficent change, however, even when it does take place, is not immediate. There is first a distinct alteration for the worse, which, unless he has been previously instructed in the matter, considerably alarms the nervous patient. At the Baths of Leuk there is a disfiguring but favourable eruption, called, if I remember right, *La Poussée*, and every one asks you, *Avez-vous la Poussée?* which, since it is not necessarily exhibited in the face, is to the modest stranger embarrassing. At our English Baths there is no such indelicate inquiry, because their effect is obvious. The visitor arrives, perhaps without the use of his hands, and after a day or two of bathing and imbibing finds he has also lost the use of his legs: this, he is told, is a very healthy sign, and one on which he is universally congratulated. 'Our waters,' say the inhabitants of these sanatoria, with conscious pride, 'find out whatever is wrong in the system, and develop it.'

Some people come to them for pleasure, or to accompany their sick friends, and try a bath or two 'for fun.' Then they are laid up at once with diseases which they had no idea were in their systems, and are told that they ought to be truly thankful for the discovery. What they know to be amiss with them is, on the other hand, for the time greatly aggravated. One of the completest (eventual) cures is said to be that of a gentleman whose neck was turned half round with the rheumatism, and such were the magical powers of the waters that in a few days it 'came round' entirely, but the wrong way, and he took a back view of the universe.

> His head was turned, and so he chewed
> His pigtail till he died,

sang Hood of the sailor, but this gentleman, far from dying, lived to see straight before him and to bless the waters. Some people, however, have not the patience to wait for the cure to take effect, but on the appearance of some unexpected and alarming symptom, and in spite of the confident assurances of the local doctors, secretly take the train for the South, more dead than alive, and telegraph to their wives (who are all for philosophy and perseverance) to follow them at leisure with their luggage.

The spectacle of the early bather returning

up the hotel garden from his ablutions is attractive to those who have only breakfast in view. At 7.30 he thought himself decently, if not picturesquely, attired in an ulster, a blazer, and a pair of flannels; but that is not his opinion as he meets the gay and glittering throng on their way to the coffee-room. In vain he affects an air of nonchalance, and such speed as his malady admits of; a rash, or something like it, which for once is not a development of the local cure, pervades his features. Other and less energetic invalids are drinking the waters out of soda-water bottles, which, it being a wet morning, they have sent down to the magic well to be filled. This is, however, a practice frowned upon by the faculty, while the early bather who, it is needless to say, goes in person for his drink wins their approving smile. Moreover, as with the case of the healing powers of a still more famous pool, precedence is a question of importance, for in the season there is a great demand for baths. First come is first served, and the midday dipper has oftentimes to wait, a process much resented by all victims of the prevailing complaint, and even others.

It is a question whether it is better that the sick and the hale at these health-resorts should dwell together or apart. At present each monster hotel contains its share of both. It is, no doubt, a hindrance to recovery and an additional weight to depression to have none but one's fellow-invalids about one; but, on the other hand, it arouses envy in the sick man's breast to see his neighbours taking sparkling wines at the *table d'hôte* while his doctor restricts him to whisky and soda. It must be confessed, however, that considerable delicacy is exhibited. At the whist-table, which is common to both parties, a player is said on one occasion to have apologised to his rheumatic companions for being able to deal—an operation performed in their case by deputy in the person of one of the hotel pages. Some of the worst cases are the most cheerful. 'As for markers,' says the jolly old colonel, who is justly the favourite of our establishment, when the whist party were waiting for them, 'except for the look of the thing, we can do without them, for we have all got our chalk-stones.'

What is touching at these health-resorts is

to see round the smooth bowling-greens the ranks of Bath chairs with their occupants evidently mindful of their own past exploits with the 'wood,' and wondering whether the waters will ever enable them to stoop to conquer again. That, and to feed the pigeons, is all that most of us are good for, but, as our cheerful colonel observes, 'feeding the pigeons is at all events better than feeding the worms.' This philosophy we all admire, but it is a very different matter when a visitor who has nothing the matter with him ventures to joke about our little ailments. Like the Greenwich pensioners of old as regarded the Hospital, we may abuse our health-resort ourselves, but exceedingly resent any criticism of it by outsiders. Some of our weaker or more impatient brethren may lack faith, but that only renders the intrusion of the avowed sceptic more intolerable. Would it be credited that, on one tempestuous morning, when we had all sent down our soda-water bottles to the life-giving spring, and were waiting for them in the great hall, a would-be facetious person had the ill-taste to quote aloud the famous Cheltenham epitaph, with the name of our health-resort substituted for that of the Gloucestershire Spa:—

> Here lies I and my two daughters,
> All through drinking of these blessed waters;
> If we had stuck to Epsom salts
> We'd not have been lying in these here vaults!

I need not point out the extreme vulgarity of the last three words, but it was the application of the thing that offended us so. Anything more improper and inappropriate it is difficult to conceive. There may have been cases where the waters may not have 'carried off' everything, as the guide-book assures us they do, but the idea of their being capable of carrying off a visitor was, we felt, most offensive. Jokers of this kind should not be admitted to hotels, or at all events be charged for at an increased tariff; but when we expressed an opinion to this effect, this facetious person declared that in his case it would have made no difference, since he was not at all a joker at home, but supposed the complaint had been dormant in his system, and that the drinking of the waters had brought it out. Our old soldier protested that it was impossible to be angry with an individual capable of thus excusing himself, but as a matter of fact we were angry.

The hotel legends illustrative of the cure are various. The most agreeable is perhaps the story of the Wreck. The Wreck was a young fellow who arrived at the watering-place a cripple and a skeleton. His youth and melancholy condition (for, of course, he got worse and worse) attracted all feminine hearts from the fourth floor to the first; they hung about his couch and helped to wheel his Bath chair; some of them read novels and some of them read sermons to him, according to their dispositions. It was understood that he was bound for an early grave, so that there could be no harm, though pity is said to be akin to love, in pitying him. In due time, however, the waters made him well, and then there were dreadful scenes. He was an honourable young man, however, and married—one at a time, of course—as many of his admirers as he could, beginning (to give the rest as good a chance as possible) with the eldest.

On the other hand, another young fellow,

apparently in the best of health, arrived at the hotel with his beloved object and her family, intending to spend a fortnight with them before his marriage. He took a glass or two of the waters, doubtless in her honour, for she was by all accounts a lass who would have been 'an excuse for a glass' of almost anything, and in ten days he was a cripple. After a season or two he not only became completely cured, but more healthy than ever, only in the meantime the lady got tired of waiting for him, and married somebody else.

They have a theory at these health-resorts that though the waters may do you no good while you are dipping and drinking, they improve you wonderfully when you get home.' This is somewhat akin to the assurance of those high-flying educationalists who tell us that though we may have learnt nothing particular when at college, it has taught us to educate ourselves after we have left it. If a patient can thus be got out of the place in a hopeful frame of mind, it is almost as good—for the health-resort—as making him well, which completes the parallel.

GETTING INTO PRINT

GETTING INTO PRINT

SOLOMON tells us that there is nothing new under the sun; but he spoke from insufficient data. When he enumerates the various vanities to which human nature is subject, he omits to mention the desire of seeing oneself in print, because that desire was born a good many years after his time. The exact date is not known, but it was probably not very much after 1252, in which year printing was invented. That there should be nothing said about this natural yearning in any ancient publication is not to the point, because each writer obviously must have obtained his wish, and no doubt forgot all about it as soon as it was gratified. It is difficult to imagine any one yearning to have his thoughts appear in black-letter; but Leigh Hunt, in his charitable, delightful way, contends that even the habit of cutting one's initials on historical memorials and on trees is not only natural but even commendable, since it arises from the desire for fame on the part of those who have no other means of obtaining it. Only a few people read blackletter and initials on trees, and in neither case was there any *honorarium* for the author. Indeed, to do it justice, the desire of seeing oneself in print has no association with the lust of gain; in its first bloom, at least, it is as far removed from all considerations of lucre as is the desire of the youthful savage for his first scalp. And yet one cannot say that the motive is solely honour and glory. There is a good deal of egotism, and perhaps not a little vanity, in the matter. As the young warrior is admired by the squaws for being 'decorated' with that proof of his prowess, so the young writer with his first 'proof' receives the congratulations of his female friends. He has emerged from the ruck of mankind, and become an author.

Upon this it may justly be observed that in nine cases out of ten he had much better not have emerged; but then, unless this had happened in the tenth case, even the man of genius would never have become an author at all. There are similar objections to marriage; but the world must be peopled, and though the great majority of us are not worth much, a few are valuable members of society, and it would be a pity to nip them in the bud. At all events here we are, and that being so, those that have brought us into the world are bound to do the best for us. The same reasoning applies to the desire of seeing oneself in print; it may be a morbid ambition, but the thing exists, and those who harbour it increase and multiply. Under these circumstances, it is perhaps only reasonable that one who has been the literary godfather of a good many beginners should offer aspirants a few words of advice.

I take it for granted that the aspiration of the would-be man of letters is of modest dimensions — that he wishes to contribute something to a periodical, and not to publish a book. Indeed, if he be a rich man, he will not, in the latter case, need any help. Any fool can bring out a book if he is able to pay for its publication. People with literary proclivities are, however, generally poor; and moreover, it must be remembered that the author of a volume need not obtain even a single reader, whereas the contributor of an article to a magazine has at least a good chance of finding some among its many subscribers. The mere seeing oneself in print, though no doubt a delightful experience, is not very satisfactory unless we can get other people to look at us.

I do not pretend, of course, to suggest the character of the composition; if that—with one exception, however—does not suggest itself to the writer, his chance is small indeed. The exception is poetry. Almost all persons who have made their mark in the world of letters have begun as poets; they echo more or less harmoniously the songs of their favourite bards; they think they are going to die young (though not before they have made themselves immortal by their touching verses), and take melancholy leave of a world with which they have not yet made acquaintance. It is very difficult to persuade these 'one-foot-in-the-grave-young-men,' as Mr. Gilbert calls them, to take any counsel from anybody. Their genius knows no law and needs no teaching. Still, I would venture to suggest to them that if they want to appear in print, they had better not, just at first, write epics, hundreds of lines of blank verse, nor indeed blank verse at all; an editor's face is apt to reflect the blank. I need hardly say that they should not write five-act plays. Translations of the *Odes* of Horace, also, perhaps they will permit me to suggest, are not recommendations in themselves on the score of novelty.

I suppose a poet would hardly think of sending his lucubrations to the *Mechanic's Magazine* or the *Political Economist*, but the prose writer in embryo knows nothing of anomaly and inappropriateness. It is quite amazing how he leaves out of the question the suitability of his contribution to the publication which he proposes to patronise; he thinks only of the harmony of his own composition, and not at all of its adaptability to the 'organ' to which he sends it. Yet this is a most important consideration. First im-

I

pressions are almost as valuable in literature as in art; and what sort of an opinion must an editor form of a contributor who has not taken the trouble to study the character of his magazine, and has perhaps even addressed it under a wrong title? To send along with his contribution a letter of several pages, containing a little biography of himself, with a passing reference to his ancestors, and concluding with his literary aspirations, is a form of self-introduction often used by the young author, but one which I do not recommend. The contribution should speak for itself. There is even a worse plan than this, namely, the calling with it in person and demanding an interview, with the object of explaining it *viva voce*. This is indeed what Artemus Ward used to call 'a high-handed outrage in Utica' to all editorial feeling. It is not to be denied that in the case of a young and pretty female contributor this scheme may have its advantages; but I protest even against that as manifestly unfair. By all means send a letter with your article, but let it be a very short one; write your name and address on your manuscript; enclose stamps, but not a stamped envelope (that is really too tempting for human nature); and, in a word, give your editor as little trouble as possible.

The question of private introductions is a difficult one. It is right to hold as a literary dogma that 'an editor has no friends'—though it seems rather hard upon him, since he makes so many enemies,—but this must be taken with a grain of salt. Of course he has friends, and unfortunately some very injudicious ones. They not only worry him often with very sad stuff of their own, but encourage *their* friends to shoot their rubbish at him. It is hardly to be expected that those who are consumed by such a passionate desire as that of appearing in print will be so chivalrous as Adelaide Procter, who, though well known to Dickens, always sent her contributions to *Household Words* anonymously and written by an amanuensis; but they should not abuse their friendship with an editor, however much they may privately abuse *him*. In nine cases out of ten he is not the proprietor of the periodical he conducts, and they should remember, in requesting him to stretch a point in their favour, that he must do it at another person's expense. One cannot expect them, being human, not to take advantage of their 'pull'; but I would counsel them to pull gently, and if the bell is not answered, not to pull more than half a dozen times.

While we are on these delicate matters, I would also respectfully suggest that a letter sent as an *avant-courier* by a total stranger, requesting to know how much the editor pays a page, is not as a rule an epistle of recommendation as regards the promised manuscript. To send a story 'by the author of' a great many other stories, which, ten to one, the editor never heard of, or to add to the writer's name 'contributor to' the *Sunday Spy*, the *Saturday Sledge-hammer*, or some other periodical little known to fame, is also a bad plan. It is something like putting A. S. S. after one's name, which, in default of the initials of some really learned or well thought of society, had better be omitted.

Unless he has really nothing else to write about, let the man who has a passion to appear in print avoid 'recollections of travel.' All the world travels nowadays, and a writer of exceptional talent is required to invest the subject with interest. To describe in detail what a bad breakfast you got at some place in Asia Minor, or how you had to wait for dinner among the Crim Tartars, is very little more interesting than the same incident in New York or London. If the writer has had an exceptional experience—was driven, for example, to *eat* a Crim Tartar—this observation of course does not apply; but your ordinary traveller, though he often bores you to death, is rarely a cannibal. Another subject to be avoided is translations. It is quite remarkable how, at a time when there is nothing extraordinary in the possession of half a dozen languages, people continue to plume themselves upon their knowledge of French and German. To make a translation interesting requires not only a good subject, but one that recommends itself to the taste of English readers, and an intelligent as well as accomplished adapter, who can free himself from trammels (the style of progression of most translations being that of jumping in sacks). But even when all is done, and done well, a translation is generally but a poor thing.

It may not unnaturally be remarked that this advice to would-be authors is mostly of the negative kind; but that is from the necessity of the case. I cannot picture to myself, though I have very often been asked to do so, the particular line that a young writer's genius may happen to take. His turn of mind may be humorous, in which case let him avoid flippancy; or dramatic, when he must steer clear of too much 'sensation,' or he will be humorous without intending it; he may be theological, artistic, or Heaven knows what. But whatever he writes about, let him write legibly. Editors are not so much in want of contributions that they will waste their eyesight over manuscripts which, twenty chances to one, will never repay their pains. Moreover, in these typewriting times there is no sort of excuse for it. For a few shillings anything can now be copied so clearly that it is almost as good as print, while a duplicate of the article is at the same time retained. If the writer loses his would-be contribution in the post, it at once becomes 'invaluable,' just as when a trout gets off one's hook we immediately persuade ourselves that it was the biggest fish in the river.

As a general rule, the best thing to which a young writer can apply his wits is a description of some personal experience of his own. The more remarkable it is, of course, the better, since the less he will have to rely upon excellence of treatment to make it interesting. It is far easier to describe than to imagine, to recall an incident to memory than to invent one. Some persons, like Single-speech Hamilton in another line, have acquitted themselves admirably in this way just once, and never entered the lists of literature again—an example not encouraging to quote, but their desire to see themselves in print at least is gratified.

The neophyte in letters should give as little introductory matter as possible; there is nothing like a preface for putting an editor out of temper. He exclaims to himself, with Hamlet, 'Why does not this fellow leave off making his damnable faces and begin?' Only a very few people can perform in literature what is called in military drill 'marking time'; the writer should make haste to get on with his story. If he can open with a striking scene, so much the better; but this necessitates a somewhat high level of interest throughout. It must not be his only dramatic situation; and he must be very careful to keep what the postboys call 'a gallop for the avenue'—something good to finish with. It disappoints an editor very much to find a narrative which had at first favourably impressed him 'fizzle out' like a spent firework. The true story-teller always keeps his 'finis' in mind, and leads up to it from the first.

I would impress also another thing upon the neophyte in story-telling—that he must have a story to tell. It is no use for him to write aimlessly and trust to 'inspiration,' as he wildly calls it, to provide him with interesting material. The mistake of the young fictionist is to narrate a series of adventures, at the end of each of which all interest ceases, and he has to begin to weave his web again, when perhaps his flies escape and never give him another chance of catching them. He makes very hard work for the reader, who has no momentum to carry him up the next hill.

The personal introduction of the writer into his story is also much to be deprecated; it will take all he knows to give *vraisemblance* to his little drama, and he should be careful not to endanger it by showing his head before the curtain. True, Thackeray did it, but we are not so curious to see every writer as we were to see Thackeray.

The placing the scene of a story in a foreign land is always disadvantageous. It may be mere ignorance which causes untravelled readers to prefer stories of their own land, but such is the fact. They feel the same want of reality in stories of foreign countries as in a fairy tale. All editors know this, and look askance at such productions. This is still more true of the historical story. Mr. Blackmore, it is true, has delighted us all with his *Lorna Doone*, and Mr. Besant with his *Chaplain of the Fleet*, but the gentleman whose desire is to appear in print is not likely to be either a Blackmore or a Besant at starting. At one time, thanks to

Walter Scott, there was a rage for stories of the middle ages, but that has utterly died out. Even genius such as dwelt in George Eliot was unable to contend against the two drawbacks of a distant scene and a distant age, as in *Romola*, which, notwithstanding its great merits, never obtained the popularity of her home novels. 'This may be a faithful picture of life and manners as they once existed,' says the reader to himself, 'but I have only the author's word for it; I prefer something of the truth of which I can judge for myself.' A very uncultured view of matters, no doubt, but not an unnatural one, and for my own part I confess I sympathise with it. Many a famous writer, such as the authors of *Hereward* and *The Last of the Barons*, for example, has broken his strong teeth over *this* file. For similar reasons, but also because it smacks of affectation and shows poverty of expression, a writer should never interlard his dialogue with French phrases; it is quite as offensive to use them in writing as in conversation. A still worse vulgarity is the frequent use of italics. It evinces a want of sense of proportion—a thing of great importance in composition—and sets an editor who knows his business almost as much against a manuscript as bad spelling.

A very common practice with young writers is to indicate the names of their localities, and sometimes even of their characters, by an initial letter. Their imagination must indeed be at a low ebb to be reduced to such a strait as this. It is difficult to interest an editor in what goes on 'at W——, in 18—,' and still more so in the amatory passages between 'Mr. A——' and 'Miss B——.' This method of expression may arise from extreme delicacy of mind; but I am afraid, as in physical matters, the delicacy involves a certain weakness. Again, it may be due to modesty that some young writers never express themselves with certainty, but always put in an 'almost' or a 'perhaps' in their statements, which has the same undesirable effect as adding water to skimmed milk. These are trifles, but it is possible that the whole contribution may be a trifle, and only preserved from rejection by its freedom from these irritating drawbacks. 'The service of the Creator,' once observed a certain divine to a younger member of the same profession, of whose acquirements he was somewhat jealous, 'stands in no need of our wisdom'; to which the other not unreasonably rejoined, 'But it still less stands in need of our folly'; and even in less important matters, such as literature, it is worth while to avoid affectation, carelessness, and insolence.

Genius has been described as 'an infinite capacity for taking pains,' and even without genius an aspirant to literary honours is likely to be successful precisely in proportion to the care and attention he gives to every portion of the work he has set himself to do. The best motto, indeed, for the disciple of literature is, 'Take pains,' and not the more frequently inculcated maxim, 'Try again.' Perseverance is in most cases a necessity; but all the perseverance in the world, and even all the taking pains, are useless unless the aspirant has some natural gift. His case is not that of Bruce's spider, who had only to try often enough to obtain his object; it is more often that of the moth in the candle, which consumes itself 'in fruitless flame.' In almost all other things the old provincial proverb, 'It is dogged as does it,' holds good; but it is not so in letters. The conclusion of the undergraduate, plucked in many examinations, who, 'at last disgusted, took and cussed it, and didn't try again,' is one which he who has a desire to see himself in print is very loath to come to. He prefers to think that there is a universal conspiracy to suppress his genius. Yet if what he writes is really good, is it reasonable to suppose that a dozen editors, one after another, would reject it, when the very thing they are looking for, for their own sakes, is a good contribution. The want of this, in fact, is almost the sole reason why so many bad ones find their way into print. The editor does not care one penny whether his would-be contributor is old or young, rich or poor, saint or sinner, but only about his article being acceptable. Nay, as one who 'knows the ropes' has well expressed it, he is 'apt to overvalue the merely readable work of an unknown hand, because even mediocrity shines out against the general average of volunteered contributions.' Moreover, there are 'dead seasons,' when good work comes sparely in, and he is obliged to provide against them by occasionally accepting what is not quite up to the mark.

Nevertheless, the inveterate persistence of the 'rejected' has to me, who have known hundreds of such cases, something very pathetic about it. They cannot understand why this passionate desire of theirs to appear in print can never be gratified; and when at last they recognise that all is over, so far as one editor is concerned, who may have rejected them with unusual tenderness, they naïvely ask him to recommend them by letter to another: 'This gentleman is not good enough for my periodical, but is admirably adapted for yours.'

There is no more unpleasant, and, too often, no more unthankful task, than, in answer to some last appeal of one who has mistaken his profession, to tell him the honest truth; it is a pill that is very difficult to silver. Yet editors have sometimes even more painful duties. A great author once found his editor looking very grave and embarrassed. 'I have got to write to a man,' he explained, 'to tell him his stories will not suit us.' 'Well, I suppose it is not the first time you have had to do that.' 'Of course not, but this is S——,' naming a writer of great eminence. The author stood aghast. 'Yes,' continued the editor, 'he has broken down; there is no more meat on his bones, and it is rather difficult to tell him so.' Terrible news indeed; and yet unless Death—a chambermaid who sometimes oversleeps herself—raps at our door in good time, news that must one day be brought to every one of us.

THE COMPLEAT NOVELIST

K

THE COMPLEAT NOVELIST

I HAVE for years been subject to inquiries from persons utterly unknown to me (except that their name is Legion) as to how fame and fortune (but especially the latter) are to be won by writing novels. The college where the art of 'How to write fiction' is to be taught, though well ventilated, is not yet, it appears, built. There are professors, but they have not regularly set to work; they resemble Ministers without portfolios, a class of statesmen the nature of whom is a puzzle to many persons; there are even books—handbooks, primers—published on this subject, but they do not seem to have fulfilled their mission as guides to the Temple of Fame. Modesty and probability alike suggest that no advice of mine will be more successful. The service demanded of me is, in fact, rather a large order. The idea seems to be that the profession of a novelist (though, Heaven knows, we are no conjurers) is similar to that of those *prestidigitateurs* who, after a performance, are prepared for a consideration to inform the curious how it is done. Still, as the inquirers are so numerous, and as that section of the public (though fast diminishing) which does not write novels seems also to take an interest in the subject, I propose to give a hint or two on it which may probably prove serviceable. The theme itself is by no means dull, and has features in it which are even amusing. I need not say that the correspondents who ask, 'How to write fiction,' though they have probably written reams of it, have published nothing. When a man—and especially a woman—has done *that*, he wants advice from nobody, and exccedingly resents it being offered. These, however, are all Peris (most of them female ones) standing more or less 'disconsolate' at the gate of Eden (situated in Paternoster Row), whose 'crystal bar' has proved immovable even to their tears.

'How shall I sit down to write a novel?' inquires one pathetically, who obviously desires instruction from the very beginning. There is a greater choice about this than she probably imagines. I knew one novelist who, while pursuing his trade, never sat down at all, but stood at a desk—which is how, not his legs, but his shoulders 'got bowed.' Another walks 'to and fro' (like the Devil) seeking for ideas. A bishop, the other day, revealed to us the fact that he always wrote on his knees; but the work, we conclude, was a devotional one, and not a novel. One popular story-teller, to my personal knowledge, used to write upon his stomach (*i.e.* lying upon it), with his reference books around him, like a sea beast among rocks.

This preliminary settled, however, my fair inquisitress asks me how to begin. This is an inquiry the importance of which is apt to be underrated, and, though an initial one, should not be the first. The first should be: 'What shall I write about?' It is amazing how many of our story-tellers, and especially of the female ones, begin story-telling without having a story to tell. They start off, often at great speed, and sometimes too fast, but in no particular direction. 'Where are you going to, my pretty maid?' is a question which, in their turn, might be asked of them. They are certainly not 'going a-milking,' if their milch cow is the public. It is fair to say, however, that almost all beginners, whether male or female, fall into this error. Yet it is only geniuses who can write brilliantly about nothing. 'There is no preparation, there is no mechanique,' is a statement only applicable to great magicians. Think how the greatest novelists have, sooner or later, had to give their attention to plot! There have been, of course, some very fine character-novels, but these have not been written by beginners; to delineate character requires above all things experience and observation. As a general rule the advice that should be given to all budding novelists is: 'Don't be in a hurry to blow. If you have no story to tell, wait till you get one.'

The necessity indeed of having the plot of one's novel—or at all events the skeleton of it—arranged beforehand, is surely as obvious, when one comes to think of it, as that of knowing the lines of a ship, or the plan of a building, before commencing their construction. Few of us, having determined to build our own houses without the aid of an architect, have not come to grief; I know one enterprising person who forgot the stairs. If you only want a bungalow—a cottage on the ground floor—of course, this doesn't so much matter; and similarly, the smaller the story the less there need be of plot; but some sort of plan to work upon—subject to alteration, and with plenty of room for additions—you must have. The question, of course, arises: How to get it? But this must be answered by the inquirer himself. It must depend upon some incident or circumstance more or less dramatic, which has made a deep impression on the writer's mind; it may have originated there (which is the better way), or it may have been communicated to it, but the impression must be deep. Moreover, it should not be recent; the longer he reflects upon it, as the cow chews the cud, the more likely he is to succeed with it. Half a dozen lines suffice in the first instance for the germ of the story. They look bald enough, but there are potentialities in them for those who can use them, just as music, the poet tells us, lies in the eggs of the nightingale. As the born story-teller dwells on them, they expand page after page. New incidents, new situations, new characters gradually present themselves as in some magic mirror. The two former may be the offspring of the imagination, but the latter should owe their being to memory: they should be studies from real life. Great care must, however, be taken to prevent recognition. The appearance, the neighbourhood, the profession of those portrayed should altogether differ from what they are in reality. Great distress of mind as respects this matter has been caused by many an undesigned coincidence, and all traces of personal resemblance should be concealed as carefully as an Indian hides his trail.

Whatever may be the merits of novels of character, it is certain that they do not appeal to the great world of readers as those do which deal with dramatic situations and incidents. As the life of the body is the blood, so the life of the novel is its 'story.' My correspondents seem to treat this as easy to procure; but they are mistaken. There are many people indeed who protest they have any amount of plots to give away; 'just the very thing to write about'; but as John Leech used to say when a poor joke was suggested to him for *Punch*: 'Admirable indeed, my dear fellow, but it does not lend itself to illustration.' Not one-tenth of the stories suggested by our friends are suitable materials for a novel.

Singular as it may appear, before the beginning of a story is attempted, the writer who wishes to do the best for himself, and is not afraid of taking pains, should fix upon the end of it. However long may be the journey, and tired may be the horses, the post-boy who has any self-respect will always 'keep a gallop for the avenue.' He is well aware of the advantage, as regards remuneration, of leaving a good impression at the last. While as for the post-boy who doesn't know his way, nor even the place for which he is bound, it is obvious that he doesn't understand his business. I am convinced that the best novels, not 'sensational' ones only, but those of sustained interest, have been composed, so to speak, backwards. The having the *denouement*, perhaps the catastrophe, well on one's mind from the first, is a precaution similar to that which is taken by a public speaker who, whatever he forgets, is careful not to lose sight of his peroration. He well knows that is what he has to lead up to, and that upon the nature of it will chiefly depend his success. However well he may have got on up to that point, if his conclusion is lame and impotent, his speech will be a failure. Moreover, the foreknowledge of the end suggests much of the proper course of events in a story. This is hardly to be understood by one who is not a novelist. Perhaps I may be forgiven the apparent egotism of an allusion to *Lost Sir Massingberd*—a small thing, but mine own—to which I venture to allude only as an illustration.

An ancient tree, which though perfect to the eye was hollow, suggested a novel method of disappearance. A man might climb into it and fall through, hands over head, without possibility of extrication. Only his muffled cries for help might be heard in the wood for hours without recognition. This was obviously not a position in which to leave one's hero, but a very good way of disposing of one's villain. The wicked baronet of the story was drawn from life; but he never would have been drawn at all except for the tree. He was buried—not in elm, if I remember right, but in oak—before he was born. In thinking the story out before putting pen to paper, the other characters introduced themselves quite naturally.

If the conclusion of a story occurs to one as striking and dramatic, it must not be put aside, of course, on the ground of its being melancholy; but as a general rule I would warn young novelists against 'bad endings'; it is their weakness to indulge in them just as it is that of young poets to rhyme about premature death. Youth has the 'trick of melancholy.' A few readers may sympathise with this feeling, but the majority exceedingly resent an unhappy termination to a story in which they have been interested. Some persons will not open a novel suspected of this drawback, and I have known even books like the *Bride of Lammermoor* to remain unread in consequence. What right has a man to pen a story like Turganieff's *On the Eve* to make generations of his fellow-creatures miserable? What lesson is there to be learned from it save the inscrutable cruelty of Fate? Who is the better—or even the wiser—for it?

Trollope was, on the whole, a kindly writer, but who does not resent the absurd scruples he puts into the mouth of Lily Dale which make the lifelong fidelity of Johnny Eames futile? Take, on the other hand, Mrs. Oliphant's equally simple story of *A Rose in June*. There is sadness enough in it, but how much more naturally and satisfactorily is the course of true love brought to its close.

At all events, whether the ending is good or bad, it ought to be concealed. There are some readers, indeed, who are so unprincipled as to look at (what used to be) the third volume first, just as children cannot keep their hands from the dessert when the soup is on the table; but this conduct is contemptible. Wilkie Collins thought it criminal. I shall never forget his distress of mind when, in the vanity of youth, I boasted to him of how I guessed the secret of *The Moonstone* at an earlier date than he had intended.

The plot of the story having been decided upon, it is advisable to make a skeleton plan of it on large cardboard, with plenty of room for the filling in of such *dramatis personæ* as are deemed appropriate to it, and any incidents which may occur to the mind as likely to be suitable and attractive. The fictitious names of the characters should be placed side by side with the real ones, that their connection should not be lost sight of, while their idiosyncrasies and other recognisable qualities should be carefully avoided. It may, I hope, not be necessary, but it is still advisable, to warn the neophyte against making use of the unfair advantage which publication gives him to satirise persons who may be obnoxious to him; this is too often done, in ignorance, perhaps, of the serious consequences that may flow from it; but it is a most cowardly proceeding, like that of striking with a deadly weapon an unarmed enemy. When a satire becomes personal it is a lampoon. Even when no harm is intended, and recognition takes place, much distress of mind may be caused not only to the person satirised but to the satirist. There was little in Charles Dickens's writings to be repented of, but it is well known that he grievously regretted his delineation of Leigh Hunt as Harold Skimpole. Hunt's peculiarities were recognised at once, and the vices of Skimpole, which were not Hunt's at all, only too readily attributed to him. Apology in such cases is useless. *Litera scripta manet*; the mischief is done.

I may here say, though it is anticipating matters, that no man who wishes to be happy in his vocation should become a novelist who is so thin-skinned or impatient of censure as to take unfavourable criticisms as a personal affront, or seek to be 'even' with the man who writes it. I have known some very unpleasant consequences arise from this foolish indignation, especially where, as often happens, it has been misplaced, and the outrage has been attributed to the wrong man. By him who aspires to be a man of letters all personalities should be avoided, and especially by the writer of fiction. If he wants to be uncivil, let him write an historical novel, and pitch into somebody who has been dead for a century or two. Matters will become much too personal with him, whether he will or no, before he has done with novel writing: it necessitates a study of his fellow-creatures that will compel him to see faults where he would far rather be blind, and things distasteful in those he loves.

As for the scene of his story, I would recommend Scott, junior (if he will allow me to call him so), not to select foreign ones, however conversant he may be with them; the taste of the British novel-reader is as insular as his dwelling-place, and he prefers to read of places he has visited, and of customs with which he is familiar. There have been some exceptions, but, as a rule, even our most popular novelists have lost something of their circulation when they have ventured on alien soil. With readers who have passed much of their time abroad, there is of course no objection to this; they may even prefer it, as awakening pleasant memories; but they are but a small minority; the others best like to read of what they are familiar with, and are in a position to pass judgment on. The case is somewhat similar to that of foreign novels: those who can read them in the language they are written in take pleasure in them; but translations of them are not popular with the less accomplished. Wherever the scene of the novel is placed, however, it is absolutely necessary for the writer to become thoroughly acquainted with it. No time, or trouble, should be grudged in this matter. It is by no means, however, necessary to stay long in the chosen locality; on the contrary, the salient points which strike one on a first acquaintance are apt to be lost through familiarity with them, and it is these which strike the reader.

To pass from 'place' to 'period' I would observe that, though of late years there has been a great resuscitation of the historical novel, it is generally a mistake for writers who would be popular to place their story in a far back time. One or two have recently made a great success in so doing, but it is given to very few to clothe dry bones with flesh. It is of course necessary to study the period, and to read much literature concerning it; and the too general result of this is to give to the composition the impression of 'cram,' of its having been 'got up' for the occasion. The story that finds most readers is almost always a tale of to-day. They like to be in a position to criticise; to say this and that is contrary or in accordance with their own experience; that they have met, or not met, the characters described; whereas for the *vraisemblance* of folks in armour who moved in society upon horseback, they are obliged to accept the author's *ipse dixit*.

Almost all young writers cast their fiction in the autobiographical form, for indeed they are generally their own heroes. This has been done a few times only with success (as in the case of *David Copperfield*), even by great authors; with small ones it is a fatal error. There is always a great deal too much about the author's boyhood, which, except to his mother, is absolutely uninteresting. 'Boys will be boys,' it is said by way of apology, and they need it. Some adults may want to have their schooldays over again, which only shows they have forgotten them—but they don't want to read of other people's schooldays. There is nothing duller than the reminiscences of boyhood, except those of girlhood. Women writers scarcely ever allow their readers to escape from these narratives. They *will* begin with their heroine in short frocks, and sometimes in long clothes. She has her skipping-rope, with which we wish she would hang herself, and her girl friends, who are as unentertaining as herself, and her 'yearnings.' She yearns through a dozen chapters, while the reader yawns. It would be such a relief if she would do something, even if it were to run away with the page. Children are charming (and so are dogs) when they leaven a story, but they should not be allowed, any more than in real life, to occupy too much of the attention. And whether in youth, or at any other period, there should be no ego in a novel. The introduction of self into it is fatal. Thackeray, it may be said, did it; but it was a mistake even in his case, and it is probable that Scott, junior, is not a Thackeray. Does he suppose that his puppets are so lifelike that it is necessary (like Bottom the weaver) to put his head outside the puppet-show to assure us that they are not really alive? Does he imagine that his tale has such a sustained interest that it can bear this solution of continuity? If he does, he possesses at least one quality which some people think is necessary to literary success—'a guid conceit of himself.'

On the other hand, he should not be afraid of expressing his opinions; while young at the trade, it is better to do so through the mouths of his characters; but if this cannot appropriately be done, let him state them, though always in an impersonal way. To students of fiction it is interesting to mark how, as authors gather strength, and gain their places in the world, they deliver their *obiter dicta* upon things in general.

I may here tell a secret, or at all events something not generally known, concerning popular, and presumably good, novelists. Sometimes, of course, their circulation wanes with their wits; old age has its natural effect upon their powers of imagination; but much more commonly their reputation decays through another attribute of old age, which is by no means unavoidable, namely, indolence. They flatter themselves they are sure of their public, which, indeed, is always faithful to them as long as can be reasonably expected, and even beyond it; and they no longer take the same pains to please as they used to do; they substitute recollection for observation, and trust to memory where they formerly drew from experience. It is irksome to them to take trouble. Now, though no definition of genius is so idiotic, and absolutely contrary to the fact, as that which describes it as 'an infinite capacity for taking pains,' if pains are not taken, even genius cannot in the end succeed, however fortunate it may be in the beginning; while if Scott, junior, is only a young person of talent and not a genius (as is possible), he may just as well hope to be a great engineer, if he takes no pains, as to be a novelist. It seems so easy to those who have never done it to succeed in fiction; story-telling appears such a holiday task to the outsider; but as a matter of fact it requires a great deal of application, observation, study, and, above all things, patience and perseverance. Only a few writers 'awake to find themselves famous,' and even these have generally had rather a long night.

The greatest bugbear in the eyes of the

young novelist is the critic. This wicked creature is credited with an irreconcilable enmity to imaginative literature, and with a disposition to dance upon the bodies of all who follow it, but especially upon the young. The exaggerated fear in which he is held is in reality caused by his victims' exaggerated ideas of their own importance. If they knew what very little displacement was caused by their plunge into fiction, they would know how brief is the effect of any comments that may be made upon it. As a matter of fact, very few people read reviews, and the impression they create seldom endures beyond the week in which they appear; one review pushes the next out of recollection, as one pellet drives out another in a pop-gun. The harm wrought by an ill-natured, or what is called a 'nasty,' review—for, of course, we are not considering a just one, to which no objection should be made—depends chiefly upon whether the author vituperated is fool enough to read it. It is quite amazing how otherwise sensible persons are tempted to do this throughout their lives. I knew one very successful author who could never withstand the temptation to read what he had already heard was an 'attack upon him,' wherever it was. He used to buy the review or newspaper—thus actually increasing the resources of his enemy,—and after having made himself thoroughly miserable with reading it, tear it into fragments. The other unpleasantness about unfavourable criticism is that one's friends always get hold of it, and perhaps send one a copy of it, explaining in a sympathetic letter how they 'deplore it.' This is scarcely what is called 'backing' on the part of one's friends. The 'Compleat Novelist' would be a misnomer indeed for a gentleman who embraces that profession with the fear of the critic before his eyes. Let him lay to heart the admirable saying, 'No man was ever written down except by himself.'

When the skeleton of his story is finished, he must be careful to avoid plumping it out by padding. He should be always marching on with his story, and never 'marking time,' like a recruit at drill. Dissertations and disquisitions should be avoided. Where his characters indulge in reflection, they should be as brief as epigrams, and, if possible, as pointed. There is nothing so tedious in fiction as a Hamlet hero.

As to the nature of the novel, that must, of course, depend upon the nature of the author, but it is certain that popularity most attends the writer who can attach Cupid to his chariot wheels. By far the majority of novel readers are the ladies, and they prefer, above all others, the love-story. It is true that some of our greatest writers, Thackeray especially, and in a less degree Dickens, have not been very successful in their treatment of this matter; but genius has no laws. I have already apologised to Scott, junior, for taking it for granted that his gift is short of genius; if it were otherwise, he needs no teaching. But it is quite curious how independent is a writer who has a speciality for describing courtship of any other attractions. Trollope, who, of course, had many other gifts, could turn out whole volumes descriptive of the tender passion. The too faithful Johnny Eames is exhibited at the feet of his inamorata, not only in one novel, but several; his courtship has continuations; yet the ladies never tired of it. In these days, popularity has been sometimes obtained upon these lines after a fashion to which it is not necessary to allude; I will not suppose Scott, junior, to be capable of seeking the bubble reputation in dirty waters, as a mudlark dives for pence. There are plenty of honest women and honourable men in the world, if he have the eyes to see them and the hand to draw them.

Still I would warn him against the diffuse descriptions of the young people whose course of true love he has set himself to narrate. It will astonish him perhaps to learn that no novelist has as yet described the appearance of a heroine so as to be recognisable by his readers; the picture of her they make in their own minds will not be the one he would fain have suggested to them. At the very best it will be only such a likeness as may be gathered from a passport. Women writers will fill a dozen pages with their heroine's exquisite features (not forgetting the lobe of her ear), and a dozen more with her dress. This I do not recommend; and as for that latter matter, though I understand it is attractive to female readers, Scott, junior, being a male, is certain to make a mess of it. Nor do I think it is advisable that he should 'pan out' too much on the scenery; as a matter of fact, this is mostly skipped, but I may add concerning it, as of the portrait-painting, unless there are very salient points about it, it fails to give the impression desired. Any one who visits the places described by even such a master of the pen as Walter Scott, must acknowledge that that is his first introduction to them; he has gained no familiarity with them through the printed page.

The chief point of a novelist's endeavours should be to give his story *sustained interest*. It is of course, necessary, in a long one, to break the thread when he introduces new scenes and characters, but it should be picked up as soon as possible, and both old and new combined in it. There are many admirable works that can be taken up and laid down at any time, but this should not be the case with a novel. The aspiration of one of our greatest writers was 'to cheat a schoolboy of his hour of play' (a much more difficult task, by the bye, than to cheat him of an hour of work, which he will cheerfully give up for almost any other occupation), and the ambition of a novelist, unless he is one of those who write 'with a purpose,' should be to—what some excellent people would call—'waste the time' of his readers; that is to say, to so fascinate them that they cannot lay his story down, or go to bed, until they have finished it; and no matter what may be his wit or wisdom, he will never accomplish this unless he has a story to tell them. And thus we come round to the point from which we started, the paramount necessity of a good plot. 'A good plot,' as Hotspur says, 'and *full of expectation*, an excellent plot.'

Lastly, neither time nor pains should be spared in the choice of title. This is very important, especially with a new writer. The same foolish persons who tell us that all the plots have been exhausted, will doubtless say that the titles also have already been appropriated. A great many of them have been so, as is evidenced by the number of novels that have had to change their names between their serial publication and their book form in consequence. They are names, of course, of unknown novels, for no one would be so impudent as to take that of a well-known one—which their authors have not even thought it worth while to spend five shillings in registering. It is pretty certain that no court of law would award damages for doing what could not be helped, and what could not but result, if it had any result, in the advantage of the person (supposed to be) injured. Still, it is advisable to take every precaution possible to avoid this duplication. The title should indicate the nature of the story without revealing its secret, and should not be a proper name, which can attract nobody. *David Copperfield* and *Martin Chuzzlewit* are attractive to us, because we are all acquainted with their contents, but they are, as titles, colourless, and excite no curiosity. When Scott, junior, has attained fame, he can call his novel what he pleases.

Some care should be also taken with the names of the characters of a novel. Matters are improving in this respect, and we seldom read such obvious titles as were at one time common in fiction, reminding us of those in the *Pilgrim's Progress*. The Faithfuls and Easies, the Gammons, the Quirks and Snaps, the Sir Harkaway Rotgut Wildfires, once so familiar to us, would now be pronounced crude and extravagant. Dickens was almost the first to escape from them; his names were all taken from real life, either from what he read over shops or in the Post Office Directory. The exception is in *Nicholas Nickleby*, where, however, there is an excellent name of the *Pilgrim's Progress* type—Sir Mulberry Hawke. Scott, junior, should take his names from the Directory, but be careful to put an out-of-the-way Christian name before them, so as to avoid the risk, if not of an action for libel, at least of some personal unpleasantness. People don't like being called 'out of their names,' but still more do they dislike their real ones stuck on to a bad character in a novel, like a lady's head on the body of a comic photograph.

In all that I have said of him, let Scott, junior, distinctly understand that I pretend to teach no method of making bricks without straw. If he has no natural turn for story-telling, no human being can give it to him; but if he has a bent that way—and not merely a passionate desire to see himself in print, which is a much commoner attribute—I have endeavoured to show him how he can utilise it—what he should give his attention to, and what he should avoid. I cannot promise him success, but I believe I have shown him the way in which he is most likely to attain it.

AN EDITOR AND SOME CONTRIBUTORS

AN EDITOR AND SOME CONTRIBUTORS

LONG years ago, 'when life and hope were new,' I received a letter from him whom Bret Harte calls 'the Master,' and who is the master still to my contemporaries in literature, praising some contribution that I had written for *Household Words*, and bidding me be of good courage. It was a kind thing to do, for his written words were literally golden, and his time very precious. Moreover, though a very young beginner, I had met with many rejections as a would-be contributor, and might well have been even despaired of by an impatient judge.

But the fact is that what made Dickens a model editor was his passionate attachment to the profession he adorned. All men of letters were akin to him, and the humblest writer, provided he could show himself fitted for the calling he had chosen, was as a younger brother. Thackeray and Trollope, though both kind-hearted men, had not this feeling, and, as editors, were not to be compared with him.

The effect of this encouragement upon myself was little short of magical. A squire of old, who had been knighted by some Bayard for small service, might have felt similarly elated, and resolute to do something really meritorious in repayment for his spurs. He would perhaps have made a vow to 'our Ladye' to perform some pious act; and I made a vow to myself that, if ever in the years to come I should find myself an editor, I would take example from the one who had, as it seemed, made a man of me.

Whether that vow was kept it is for others to say; but I certainly was always in sympathy with those who strove, literally enough, to 'make their way through the press,' and win a name for themselves at the pen's point in the lists of literature. To narrate my experiences, which extended over forty years, would fill a volume; but I have set down one or two that occurred in connection with my younger contributors, who naturally always interested me the most.

In no case have I exaggerated the facts, but as these neophytes have become more or less well known in literature, I have so transposed matters as, while apparently making identification easy, will render it impossible even to the parties themselves.

Of course most contributors are personally unknown to their editor—though that is never the fault of the rejected ones, who always believe in the virtue of an interview, so that the poor editor is obliged to employ a sort of 'chucker out' to keep himself private—he has to make a picture of them in his mind, gathered from the nature of their articles.

On several occasions I had had some very bright sketches of country life from a young sportsman who, though he was mostly on horseback, seemed to have eyes about him for other things than horses and hounds. Then he sent me a short story of military life, a little erring, as was to be expected in a youngster, upon the side of fastness—too much cigar smoking and too many brandy-and-sodas

—but very graphic and entertaining. As my people were mostly military, it interested me more perhaps than it would have done others, and it interested *them*—which it was rather difficult for any story-teller to do—and thereby proved its genuine character.

I was rather pleased when the young fellow wrote that he was coming up to town to see me, and I made him an appointment for that purpose.

At the hour arranged for I was annoyed by my confidential clerk bringing me in a card with 'Miss Norman' on it. I said, 'I do not know the lady, and you are well aware that I do not see people who have not an introduction.' 'She is very ladylike, sir,' he answered, 'and pretty.' It was a wrong remark for him to make, of course, since it almost suggested that good looks were a passport which should be reserved for true merit; but I said I could give her two minutes.

Accordingly she was ushered into the hall of audience, an apartment, by the bye, on the third floor, and always in a state of litter. She was comely enough, but I at once explained to her that my time was precious, and that I had made an appointment for that very hour. 'You will show Mr. Marchmont up, when he comes, at once,' I added to the clerk, with significance.

'But I *am* Mr. Marchmont,' said the lady.

You might have knocked me down with a feather.

Nothing she had written had given me the least hint of her being of the fair sex. Nay, what would to my mind have done away with all suspicion, had I entertained any, was that she had always taken my alterations in her sketches with the greatest good-nature. As a rule, if you venture to hint that this or that falls short of excellence in a lady's contribution, she is surprised, and by no means pleased; 'any other fault she could have imagined in her composition, but you must excuse her remarking that the paragraph in question was written with particular care, and, if excised, the whole article would be spoilt.' Miss Norman had acquiesced in every suggestion, and never remonstrated even at a deletion.

Her father kept hounds, her brothers were

in the army, and her writings had taken colour from their red coats. She had felt that if she wrote as one of her own sex, there would be a doubt of her knowing what she wrote about, so she adopted the pseudonym of 'John Marchmont.' By that name she afterwards became known to a large public, who is as much deceived up to this very day as I was.

For some time, though intermittently, I had been receiving certain sketches of London life in the East-End, of which I thought very highly. It was long before the days when 'slumming' became fashionable. The place was a *terra incognita* to the majority of our readers, and the articles had attracted much attention. They were written by one James Harrison, evidently a man of education and refinement, and yet showed an acquaintance with his subject—how the very poorest live—which spoke volumes either for his philanthropy or his love of adventure.

I received these articles at long intervals, as if he seldom visited the places in question; but when he did so, he evidently investigated them with great thoroughness, and described them with a realism that in less delicate hands might easily have been offensive. He always wrote, however, with good taste, though not perhaps with that sympathetic pity with which a man, presumably of good position, should regard the privations of his less fortunate fellow-creatures.

I had a good deal of correspondence with him, and had more than once asked him to call upon me, but he had never done so. His letters, and the cheques they enclosed, were invariably addressed to him at some post-office instead of a private house; and whenever he was thus communicated with, I noticed there was a long interval before we heard from him again; this is unusual with young contributors —he had told me he was young—upon whose imagination cheques have generally a prolific effect: they begin to write at once, on the receipt of them.

One day my clerk came into the room with a troubled face, as though something unpleasant had happened; he said that a man had called that morning before my arrival, giving the name of Harrison, and that he had been sent away, but was now returned.

'Why had he been sent away?' I asked, 'since you knew that I wished to see him?'

'Well, sir, I thought he was an impostor'—of whom indeed we have many—'but since he has come again——'

'Show him in,' I interrupted, much displeased that discourtesy should have been offered to so valued a contributor; yet when he entered I felt that the clerk had had every excuse for his conduct. I thought for the moment that I was in the presence of a street beggar.

The man was in threadbare black, without a sign of linen about him; his buttonless coat was fastened across his chest with a pin, not because it was cold, for it was summer, but obviously to conceal the absence of a shirt; the collar was turned up, doubtless for the same reason; his shoes were patched, and the sole of one of them was loose, and flapped as he moved. Yet the voice was singularly gentle, though rather hoarse, in which this scarecrow observed with pathetic cynicism: 'You have expressed a wish to see James Harrison; here he is.'

From that moment I had no doubt of his

identity. I offered him a chair, and he sat down with his hat—such a hat!—in his hand, and looked at me with earnest eyes. They were not bright eyes, yet they had keen intelligence; his face, though pale and haggard, had a pleasant expression; his head had but little hair on it, yet his whole expression was youthful, the remains of a wasted youth.

'I have not had the pleasure of a contribution from you for some time,' I said.

'No,' he answered, with a smile. 'Your last cheque, you see, was a larger one than usual. So I had to run through it. However,' with a rueful look at his clothes, 'I have done it at last; so thoroughly indeed that I have not a copper to buy ink and paper with, so I had to come to you after all.'

He had evidently put off the evil day, on which he had to exhibit his degradation, as long as possible.

'Do you mean to say you have literally not a penny?'

'I have not a *farthing*,' he replied, with a sort of chuckle that was far more pathetic than a sigh.

'And are the experiences you have written

for me not only real ones—of which I am well convinced—but your own experiences?'

'They are. I have plumbed the depths of human misery.'

His story was distressing, but he had no complaint to make; he seemed to well understand that he owed all his misfortunes to himself. He was naturally idle, and would only work when compelled to do so. All his money had been spent on his education, so that for years he lived from hand to mouth. Of late years he had taken to opium-eating, which had destroyed what little remained of energy. Yet he retained his wits.

A ten-pound note had quite a magical effect on him; he came to dine with me the next day at a restaurant—I did not venture to ask him to the club—a well-dressed and intelligent young fellow, and a very interesting companion. I got him a situation on a newspaper, where he stayed six months. Then he 'went under' again, emerged fitfully for a few years, and eventually fell a victim to his drug.

One of the most common faults of literary contributors is bad handwriting; how can they expect even the kindest of editors to wade through their hieroglyphics in search of buried merit? On the other hand, it is true that some editors share this unfortunate drawback, and I have been accused of it myself.

My enemies called my caligraphy a scrawl, while my friends confined themselves to saying that my telegraph hand was better than my writing hand. Sometimes I have had letters from a contributor saying he had received my obliging communication, but could not gather from it whether his article was accepted or rejected. Of course, these people are very stupid; 'the clearest hand,' says Goethe, 'cannot be read by twilight,' but when I am writing to lady contributors I always take great care to be distinct, because they always give themselves the benefit of the doubt whenever there is one.

I had on one occasion received from a young lady in the country a charming set of verses, which I had hastened to acknowledge. Editors get so much poetry, and almost all bad—when people write in verse they seem to think that they are inspired, and therefore above criticism;

so that when anything really good comes of this kind, it is very welcome, and we write to say so. Under such circumstances a gushing answer generally comes by return of post, and editor and contributor join themselves into a mutual admiration society.

But in this case I got no reply. This so amazed me that after a while I wrote again, expressing a hope that my first communication had not miscarried. It had been only a postcard, such as I usually send when accepting small poetical contributions, but I had always found it sufficient for its purpose. This young poetess, however, was not, it seemed, so easily satisfied; she appeared to think a postcard beneath her dignity, for in her reply she enclosed the one I had sent to her.

'Sir, the cause of my silence was that I saw no sufficient encouragement in your communication, enclosed, to offer another contribution.'

My postcard was as follows: 'I hope to make use of your pretty verses.' Not an elaborate eulogy, it is true, but perfectly polite and appreciatory.

A friend happened to call upon me while I sat with this inexplicable letter in my hand.

'What do you think of this?' I said, giving it to him to read. 'Poetesses are kittle cattle to deal with, are they not?'

'But you were not civil to the lady,' he replied. '"I cannot make use of your silly verses" was downright rude.' *That* was what he had made my postcard out to be, and so had the poetess! I had never had the fact of my handwriting being but indifferent brought home to me before.

The great happiness and crowning success of an editor's career is, of course, the discovery of genius. Like gold, though it is sure to be found sooner or later, its early recognition depends on its detection by an expert. I do not say that I was a better assayer than my neighbours, but I was certainly very fortunate in my 'finds.'

There are some authors who are to me 'as captain is to subaltern,' whom I had the pleasure of raising from the ranks, and who still, like all generous minds, exaggerate the obligation. I was their Master of the Ceremonies, and introduced them to the public a few weeks earlier perhaps than they would have introduced themselves; that is all.

And there are others, alas! who gave me the same opportunity, but I did not take advantage of it.

The best editor is he who makes fewest mistakes. After all, though naturally the successful contributors excite greater interest, the less successful ones arouse more sympathy, if at least they have any merit in them. A dullard is out of place in literature, and should be courteously but firmly discouraged: here and there they make a hit—an 'outer,' never a 'bull's-eye'—and they think fame and fortune are within measurable distance, but they never see either.

Their pleadings would move a heart of adamant, but not an editor's. The reason is— and let all would-be contributors lay it to heart —that his magazine is not his own but his proprietor's; he must be just before he is generous, because if otherwise he will be giving away other people's money—a very expensive sort of charity.

Some contributors will write about a rejected contribution, when it would be so much better to treat it as spilt milk—wipe it up, and say no more about it. One unfortunate young lady wrote to me: 'How could you, *could* you, return my story by the five-o'clock post? You *must* have known I should get it the last thing in the evening, and be kept awake by the thought of it all night.' Whereas the consideration in question had never entered my mind.

One piece of advice to all literary aspirants I would particularly offer. Do not send a letter to the editor longer, or even so long, as the contribution itself. He does not want to hear that your contribution has been written three times over, or that it represents your best thoughts for years, or even that it has been written with your life-blood. He has heard all that and more from fifty other young gentlemen and ladies.

A LITERARY JUBILEE

N

A LITERARY JUBILEE

BARON TAUCHNITZ, of Leipzig, has issued a jubilee volume (*Fünfzig Jahre der Verlagshandlung Bernhard Tauchnitz*, 1887) in commemoration of his fifty years' connection with English authors. It seems but yesterday that he published a somewhat similar record on the appearance of his two-thousandth volume, but in the meantime his collection has been increased by five hundred works. A hundred and sixty-five of the whole series have been contributed by American authors, thirty of whom have served under the Baron's banner. His English host numbers no less than two hundred and seventy-six. There is a notion abroad, or rather at home, that English authors deprive no pecuniary advantage from their connection with the great Leipzig firm, but it is due to Baron Tauchnitz to acknowledge that he has always remunerated them even before the existence of international copyright, and when there was no legal necessity for him to do so. In literary matters it is not necessary to be poor and honest; one may be honest and still successful (American papers, please copy), and the Baron's case is a case in point. The volume is by no means a mere catalogue of names famous in literature; they are all there, of course, but the series is being constantly supplemented by new authors, and upon the whole with a judgment that does credit to the recruiting sergeant. The popularity of a writer in his own country of course ensures his appearance in the Tauchnitz edition; but in not a few cases Leipzig has recognised his merits even before London, and this recognition stamps him with the hall-mark of success.

It is popularly supposed that the Baron's continental series is read only by the travelling English, yet these form but a small portion of its public; it is exported everywhere, except to England and English colonies. The author himself, upon signing a certain formula to satisfy the custom-house, can procure as many copies as he pleases; but every one else who imports a copy into England breaks the law. He also hurts the English author, but I am sorry to say this does not weigh much with the British traveller, who finds the Tauchnitz edition, he says, 'so handy'—so easy, he also means, to smuggle. We have seen a whole library of Tauchnitz editions—though not, of course, his own books—in a publisher's drawing-room. It is the ladies, however, who are the greatest sinners in this way. A charming young literary smuggler was bringing home with her a Tauchnitz novel from Antwerp the other day, and made acquaintance with an agreeable stranger on the way, to whom she confided her nefarious intention. At London Bridge he reciprocated her frankness by informing her that he was a custom-house officer, and demanding that the volume should be given up.

'But I have not finished it yet,' she murmured pleadingly.

'Where have you got to?' he inquired.

She pointed with her taper finger. Gently taking the book from the fair contrabandist, he tore away what she had read and threw it into the river, returning the portion that was so precious to her with the customary bow. This was a man with some notion of duty; but I am afraid such crimes are only too often winked at. This carelessness, and the fact that those who buy English books abroad do not buy them at home, complete all that is to be urged against the Continental Series; otherwise the result of his connection with the Baron to the English author is not only gainful, but, as is abundantly evident from the testimony of his own letters, exceedingly agreeable to him.

It is seldom, indeed, that a book of such modest pretensions has the literary value which this jubilee volume possesses. There are extracts in it from the correspondence of all the famous dead authors, which are in the highest degree interesting. Though confined to one subject, many of them are very characteristic, and certainly go far to disprove the popular notion that the relations between author and publisher must needs be antagonistic. It is well to remember that, though there is now international copyright[1] there was none when

---

[1] As matters now stand, the Tauchnitz editions are as fully established by English law as any other.

Bernhard Tauchnitz first began his undertaking, and that he could have commenced it 'without the authority and sanction of English authors.' He says, indeed, in his original prospectus: 'Allow me to remark that I, as well as any other publisher in Germany, have at present the right to embark in such undertakings without any permission from the authors; and that my propositions arise solely from a wish thereby to make the first step towards a literary relationship between England and Germany, and towards an extension of the rights of copyright, and to publish my editions in accordance with those rights.' He paid for them from the very first; and that 'honesty is the best policy' can be gathered from all that follows. Mr. George Henry Lewes, for example, writes to him in 1847: 'As to remuneration, from your having transmitted English authors an *honorarium* at the time when no law of copyright rendered such an action imperative, I have conceived such an idea of your liberality and probity as to leave it to you to send me whatever sum you consider the success of the work' (*Ranthorpe*) 'may justify.' It is plain that this confidence was not misplaced, for in a communication written twenty-seven years afterwards on behalf of George Eliot, he writes: 'Both Mrs. Lewes and myself preserve such agreeable recollections of you, and of our relations with you, that it will be at all times a pleasure to receive any direct communications from you, either on the subject of our books or anything else.' In another note, in speaking of the reprinting of *Deronda*, he says—which will be read with some surprise—that 'its success in England has greatly exceeded *Middlemarch*.' Let us, however, take these literary financial communications in their alphabetical order. The amounts paid are not stated (which we confess is tantalising), but it seems certain that they have given satisfaction to the British author for a long series of years. Harrison Ainsworth writes in 1844 (eight years before international copyright was established): 'I consider your offer of . . . very liberal, and in accepting it I beg to tender you my best thanks, not so much for the amount as for the praiseworthy spirit by which you are actuated.' In the same year he writes—what seems now strange enough—'The success of my magazine' (the *New Monthly*) 'has been decided' (decisive?). 'Its sale is now second only to that of *Blackwood*. In 1856 he indites a very pretty letter about his *Flitch of Bacon, or the Custom of Dunmow*, which he inscribes to the Baron and his wife:—

'In dedicating my little book to you and Madame Tauchnitz, I selected for that dedication the happiest couple I knew; they happened at the same time to be amongst my best friends. ... It may amuse you to know that my tale has been the means of reviving the obsolete custom of Dunmow. I have promised to give a flitch of bacon to any couple who can make out their claim to it next June, and if you and Madame Tauchnitz should by accident be in England at the time I shall present it to you.'

In 1881 we find Ainsworth disposing of his last novel, *Stanley Brereton*, in the same friendly manner after a business connection of seven-and-thirty years—a fact the more noteworthy since more than one continental series had been started in opposition to that of the Baron in the meantime.

Lady Blessington is not the only one of the Baron's authors who is given to draw comparisons, but in her case it seems more curious to us now than in that of others. 'I hope,' she writes in 1844, 'you will not think me unreasonable in expecting the same remuneration for my work that my friend Sir Edward Bulwer Lytton is to receive.' She is speaking of *Strathern*. We wonder how many people remember *Strathern*. Bulwer (afterwards Lord Lytton) appears to have been a very prudent romancer. His eye, though sometimes ' in a fine frenzy rolling,' is kept in business matters on the main chance. 'It is possible,' writes this sanguine novelist in 1848, 'that the United States of America may grant us a law of copyright, in which case I might be unable to sanction any foreign reprint; and I could not sacrifice my chance of a copyright there, which would be at least as valuable to me as in my own country. . . . This I cannot forgo.' Matters, however, seem to have been satisfactorily arranged, for in 1872 we find him assuring the Baron, 'I certainly should not think of dealing with any other publisher for the continental edition.' He speaks of the

New Timon as having had an immense sale in England—'larger than any other poem since Byron'—and of *King Arthur* as his 'best and most durable work, whether in prose or verse.'

Carlyle appears to have kept quite a little stock of honey for the great Leipzig bee-master. 'I am not willing to trespass further,' he says, 'on such munificence of procedure.' And again in 1869: 'No transaction could be handsomer on your part, and you may believe me I am very sensible of it. The money account concerns me; please attend to that as already said. Friendliness and help cannot be paid, but money can and always should.' In writing to his foreign friend the Chelsea philosopher does not seem to trouble himself much about his English.

With Dickens, of course, the Baron had a very extensive connection, and their correspondence proves it to have been of a kind agreeable to both parties. It has been said that Dickens was a sharp man of business, but only by those who tried to cheat him. His genial and generous disposition made him apparently an easy prey, and his would-be plunderers, finding that this was not the case, resented the failure of their attempts exceedingly. When dealing with honest men he was as trustful as a child. 'I cannot consent,' he writes, 'to name the sum you should pay for *Great Expectations*; I have too great a regard for you, and too high a sense of your honourable dealings, to wish to depart from the custom we have always observed. Whatever price you put upon it will satisfy me.' And again: 'The first number of my new story, to be completed in twelve numbers' (which, alas! it never was, for it was *Edwin Drood*), 'will be published on the last day of this month. Your terms shall be mine, and I will most readily accept them if you will kindly state them.' In the same too sanguine spirit he hints of a new series of his *Uncommercial Traveller*: 'It is finished for the present, but I may very probably write a new series under the same title by and by.'

The Disraeli letters are among the most characteristic in the collection. 'It is with extreme satisfaction,' he writes concerning *Coningsby*, 'that I have assented to your wish to prepare an edition for continental circulation, and especially for the German public. The sympathy of a great nation is the most precious reward of authors, and an appreciation that is offered us by a foreign people has something of the character and value which we attribute to the fiat of posterity.'[1]

Of *Contarini Fleming* he writes in 1845: 'This book was published anonymously twelve years ago, has been long out of print, and has been for these last few years in great demand. It is a work highly adapted to the Germans' (one wonders why; the reasons are perhaps judiciously withheld), 'and is adorned by a portrait of the author.' Neither the author nor his little weaknesses are in his case lost in the politician. 'I have been much on the Continent during the last year' (1856), 'and have found great and frequent complaints of the omission of many of my works in the reprints which you have published of those productions. I have often intended to write to you on the subject, but the great pressure of

---

[1] Like most of Disraeli's good things, this remark is unhappily not original. John Forster is presently found using the same remark, but attributing it to its proper source: 'A foreign country is, *as Lord Bacon says*, as another age.'

affairs has always prevented me; probably the fault is mine, as I ought, perhaps, to have furnished you as heretofore with corrected copies, but the Revolution of 1848 seemed to terminate these literary speculations, and since then I have always been too busy. . . . The works omitted' (*Venetia, Vivian Grey*, and *Henrietta Temple*) 'are some of them most eagerly sought at home.' In 1871 he writes: 'I am gratified to hear of the success of *Lothair* under your auspices. I am glad to say that Messrs. Longman can give you a similar report in England, and our American brethren are not behindhand in public appreciation.' In the same year he writes: 'What are called "lives" of me abound. They are generally infamous libels, which I have invariably treated with utter indifference. Sometimes I ask myself, "What will Grub Street do after my departure? who will be there [there be?] to abuse and to caricature?" I am very busy, and rarely write letters, but I would not use the hand of another to an old friend.' On removing to Curzon Street in 1881, he writes: 'I no longer dwell in the house in Park Lane where I once had the pleasure of receiving you, but I am very near the rose and smell of it.'

Mrs. Gaskell is found complaining of the injury serial publication does to her novels: 'I am writing a good deal in addition to the last quarter of the story' (*North and South*) 'which had to be very much compressed and spoiled to suit the purposes of *Household Words*.' On the other hand she expresses her sorrow that another of her stories in its volume form is too short for the Baron's purposes: 'I am very sorry, but alas! I had no more to say, having at last married Eleanor happily.'

There are letters from Hawthorne, and Washington Irving, and Longfellow.[1] The last-named writes: 'I hope that the *Tales of a Wayside Inn* may be as successful in Germany as you anticipate. . . . You will, I think, be glad to know that they have had a great sale in this country: the first edition of 15,000 copies has been exhausted, and a second of 5000 published.' 'Your very generous ad-

---

[1] In the case of American authors the Baron of course undertakes that their books shall not be exported to the States.

dition,' he afterwards writes, 'to the original sum agreed upon between us is pleasant to me, less for the sum itself than for the trait of character it reveals in you, and the proof of your liberal way of dealing'; and again: 'I hasten to acknowledge your cheque, and to thank you for this recognition of silent international copyright.'

Charles Lever's letters are more frank than those of his brother authors. 'I am aware,' he says, 'that the fact cannot in any way affect your view of the matter, but it is as well I should mention—what, after all, is the only test of an author's actual repute and standing in his own country, viz. the money value of his writings—that for this same story I receive a sum little short of three thousand pounds.' The story was the *Knight of Gwynne*, which, it may be noticed, is an extremely long one. There is nothing more fallacious than the comparison made between the sums earned by authors past and present without taking the length of their works into consideration. Dickens, Thackeray, Lever, and George Eliot often wrote novels that would make double those of the ordinary three-volume type. Of the portrait of himself prefixed to *Jack Hinton*, Lever writes: 'It is not—at least so say my friends—a resemblance, and I can myself assure you that I do not squint, which it does abominably. I believe such things are usually given to the world far less from any desire of the public to perceive the author than from the author's own desire to be seen. I must confess I have no longings on this subject, and believe my trash will read just as well without the assistance of my countenance.' He expresses a wish to see *The Confessions of Con Cregan* in the Leipzig edition. 'It was, though unacknowledged by me, one of the most successful of my novels.' He also refers to *Horace Templeton* as being his, the paternity of which we believe has not been publicly acknowledged even yet.

Charles Kingsley writes: 'I may say that *Hypatia*, from what both Bunsen and his Excellency Von Usedom have told me in stronger terms than I shall repeat, ought to have a good sale in Germany—better than in England.'

Macaulay's correspondence with the Leipzig

house is, in comparison with that of his brother authors, quite voluminous. 'I am glad,' he writes in 1863, 'that the first edition of my essays has gone off. I wish that I could tell you when my *History of William the Third* will be published; but I am almost as ignorant about that matter as you can be. The road seems to lengthen before me as I proceed.' In 1856 he writes: 'I am perfectly satisfied with your account of our venture. My success here has been very great, I might also say unprecedented. I have already received £20,000 from Messrs. Longmans. I am ashamed to think how many better writers have toiled all their lives without making a fifth part of that sum.'[1]

Of the proposal that he should write an account of English literature of the nineteenth century, he says: 'A complete and highly finished account would occupy me many months, a hasty sketch would do me no honour. I should not choose to take upon myself the

---

[1] To Macaulay Baron Tauchnitz paid the largest *honoraria* for the continental edition of his works; to Lord Lytton the largest *honorarium* for any single romance.

business of estimating the merits of my contemporaries; it would be quite impossible for me to speak the truth without inflicting pain and making enemies.' So one would think; and yet there are people to be found who insist upon the advantage—to the general public, I suppose, to whom a quarrel between literary men has all the charm of the old cock-fights—of 'signed criticism.'

Among the many 'forgotten fights' must be reckoned Mrs. Norton's letter to the *Times*, complaining of continental piracy. She seems to have given herself little trouble about the facts of the case, and to have been in a most ladylike state of ignorance about her arrangements even with her own publishers. 'I have received your letter last night. That letter contained the first information I have ever received concerning the sale of my copyrights. I did not know, what you state, that the international copyright with Germany prevented the possibility of piracy. I did not know that you had paid for author's work both before and since such copyright. I did not know that my novels had been sold you by publishers. I attacked the system as I supposed it to exist; I regret the discussion.' Later on she says: 'I have had much greater success than novel-writing could give me in political writing, and in the discussion of laws that affect women in England.'

The most curious, and certainly the most characteristic, letters of all are those of Charles Reade. '*Christie Johnson* and *Peg Woffington*,' he writes, 'belong to that small class of one-volume novels of which England produces not more than six in a century. In the compass of one volume they contain as many characters and ideas as the good three-volume novels, and their fate is as distinct from that of the mere novel as is their reputation in England and America.'

Again: 'If you prefer to pay me a fixed sum or a share of the profits, I do not care. I know that I am in the hands of a just and liberal dealer: only this I beg—let me be paid according to my sale. For instance, if you sell fewer copies of me than of Mr. Thackeray, pay me less; if you sell more, pay me more. . . . Your collection is a noble one; it contains many authors who are superior to me in merit and reputation, but it also contains the entire works of many writers who do not come up to my knee.'

Thackeray's correspondence is also characteristic. He writes in 1856: 'Your letter of the 26th March has only just found me on my return from America, where I made a prosperous voyage, though I have not quite reached the sum of five hundred thousand dollars, which the *Allgemeine Zeitung* states to be the present amount of my savings. Don't be afraid of your English; a letter containing £ is always in a pretty style.' Curiously enough, he is the medium of introducing Reade to the Baron as 'the author of *Christie Johnson* and other most popular stories.' In 1857 he writes: 'I shall leave the agreement for a new book' (*The Virginians*) 'to your discretion entirely, premising that my publishers here pay me twice as much for it as for *The Newcomes*.'

The last deceased author whose letters are quoted in this interesting volume is Trollope. He writes, in 1872, from New York: 'My dear Baron Tauchnitz,—On arriving here yesterday

I find by the *New York Morning Herald* that I had compromised my long lawsuit with you by accepting from you an enormous sum that made my mouth water. It is odd that they should now for a second time pick me out as the object of litigation, as I never had any contention with any publisher; though, either on my own account or that of others, I suppose I have had more dealings with publishers than any man living.'

There is a general notion that Baron Tauchnitz only publishes English works; this, however, is only a small portion of his undertaking; he publishes works in Greek, Latin, German, French, and Hebrew; a collection of German authors, of French classics, of Grecian and Roman classics, of logarithmic handbooks, of jurisprudence and of theology (including the Fathers). Besides these there are dictionaries and miscellaneous works, and excellent Series for the Young in English. In 1869 Baron Tauchnitz dedicated his thousandth volume to 'my English and American authors, as a token of esteem for the living and a tribute to the remembrance of the dead.' In 1881 he celebrated the publication of his two-thousandth volume by a history of English literature in the reign of Victoria, with facsimiles of the signatures of all the authors, photographed from their correspondence or agreements; and now he crowns the edifice of his labours with this jubilee volume—a record not only interesting in itself, but illustrative of good feeling between a publisher and his authors apparently unbroken for fifty years.

VALE!

VALE![1]

THE saddest word known to our tongue, though it be a blessing in brief, is 'Goodbye'; and we have all to say it. There must be pathos indeed about it, since, in my case at least, it moves that synonym for hardness, the heart of an Editor. For more than half my life I have followed that detested calling, and shall perhaps after all die in my bed. It is superfluous to assassinate a tyrant, however hateful, after his abdication. In the thirteen years, however, that I have been privileged to conduct *The Cornhill*, there have been many halcyon days when the Rejected Contributor has abstained from menace, and even from complaint. I only wish to state what will be believed, but on some occasions he has actually acknowledged I was right to decline his lucubrations. Now that my little

[1] Mr. Payn's editorial farewell.

bouts with him are over, I confess that I have a tenderness for him. What patience (up to a certain point) does he exhibit; what amazing perseverance, what hoping against hope, until despair sets in and he perceives that the return of his MSS. from all quarters of the globe indicates a universal editorial conspiracy! It is then that he becomes dangerous —a matter, however, which no longer concerns me, but my esteemed successor. I am speaking, of course, only of the Rejected Contributor whose contributions are never accepted, and never will be. The member of every other profession sooner or later finds that he is unfitted for it—a square man in a round hole, —and if it be possible he gets out of it; but he who thinks he has 'a calling' for Literature remains in that delusion for ever. I have known a man, who could get nothing printed in his lifetime, compose the epitaph to be engraved on his tombstone, and leave the money for that purpose. It might not have been publication, but it was a permanent record of his literary gift.

The R. C.'s position is a truly pathetic one,

and I am thankful to think that, though I have been unable to comply with his requests, I have been as gentle with him, where it was possible, as though I were fanning a sleeping Venus. It was not always possible. When he demands admittance, for example, on the ground that his wife's sister married our second cousin, one is obliged to tell him that one's literary judgment cannot be interfered with by the ties of blood. Even when he states, as the stage direction says, 'with meaning,' that his aunt is a duchess, we can only say we cannot help it, and that she can't help *him*. He is most irritating when he flatters himself he is combining modesty with conciliation, and tells us that though his contribution may not be of a first-class character, he thinks, without vanity, that 'it is at least superior to most of the productions he has seen in our respected periodical.' He may be injudicious, but he is seldom cantankerous, and I doubt if at the bottom of his heart he really believes that his disappointments are caused by malignity. I am well aware that I am henceforth of absolutely no account with him; a Lord Mayor after his year of office, or a Bishop's widow, is not more completely off his or her pedestal than is an extinct editor in his eyes, but I shall always wish him well; there is not a more piteous sight than that of a man struggling with insurmountable adversity. 'Tis not in mortals to command success, nor in some, alas! to deserve it.

The bright side of an editor's life is of course where the Accepted Contributor shines on it. To one who is a true lover of Literature it is a pleasure indeed to see the nugget sparkling in its bed; to be able to tell the worker that he has not toiled in vain, that fame, and perhaps fortune, lie before him. To see the fire of hope kindle in young eyes is a sight to gladden old ones, and it has been my good fortune many times to see it. It is one of the attributes of a generous nature to exaggerate a kindness, but the extent to which this is carried by literary folk is wellnigh incredible. In no other calling are such vast returns of gratitude obtained from so small an investment of assistance. It is not possible in these days for genius to be stifled in the bud, but it is a privilege indeed to encourage it to flower. That is why when 'we' resign our editorships we are not resigned: our life has lost one of its purest pleasures. There is, however, a noble consolation: the pupils of one generation become our masters in another, but they remain for ever our friends. It is to these, with a sad heart, yet full of pleasant memories, that I bid FAREWELL.

One other word, and I have done. There are two things about my departure that may well console even a sick man. The one, that ill health and not ill humours, no weakening of my long bond of friendship—a cable without a kink—with the founder of *The Cornhill* divorces me from my occupation: and the other, that of my successor all men have a good word to say. May health attend him, and especially a fine circulation!

WORKS BY JAMES PAYN.

'A little masterpiece.'—NATIONAL OBSERVER.

Crown 8vo. limp red cloth, 2s. 6d.

THE DISAPPEARANCE OF GEORGE DRIFFELL.

THE SPEAKER.—'Mr. Payn has never written a more excellent story.'

THE ATHENÆUM.—'Uncommonly well told. . . . The book is full of those good spirits and those dashes of fun which have lighted up all his writings.'

THE DAILY NEWS.—'The story evolves through a sequence of ingeniously devised and vividly presented scenes, and the dialogue has unfailing point and wit. The interest holds us to the end.'

THE CHRISTIAN WORLD.—'A capital story, told in the artistic photographic style in which Mr. Payn is a master.'

'Replete with good stories.'—THE TIMES.

SECOND EDITION. Crown 8vo. 3s. 6d.

GLEAMS OF MEMORY;
WITH SOME REFLECTIONS.

THE WORLD.—'Of all the personal books that have appeared of late years, Mr. James Payn's "Gleams of Memory" is the most attractive. . . . It is not a book to be analysed or criticised; it is to be read, liked, and simply believed.'

PUNCH.—'Within its modest limits of space will be found not only some of the best stories of the day, but stories the best told. Not a superfluous word spoils the gems.'

THE SATURDAY REVIEW.—'Mr. Payn's "Gleams" are gleams of sunlight; memories of old laughter echo through his unaffected pages.'

'One of the pleasantest books that has appeared for some time.'
PALL MALL GAZETTE.

Fcp. 8vo. limp cloth, 2s. 6d.

SOME LITERARY RECOLLECTIONS.

THE ATHENÆUM.—'To say that Mr. Payn is seen at his best in the book is as much as to say that it is remarkably pleasant reading. The stories it contains are not all new. . . . But, old and new, the stories are all well told. . . . And then the spirit of the book is eminently generous and gay. . . . In brief, his book is one of those which, like that of Maxime du Camp, if for somewhat different reasons, leave a good taste in the mouth. . . . For that reason, if for no other, it should have readers in abundance.'

THE SATURDAY REVIEW.—'In a season of biographies and reminiscences Mr. Payn's "Recollections" have several peculiarities of their own. First, they are short —we wish they were longer. . . . Again, Mr. Payn's Memories are all good-natured. . . . Thirdly, Mr. Payn's Memories have nothing to do with politics. . . . Mr. Payn's "Recollections" are quite full of anecdotes of authors, editors, publishers, yea, even of publishers' readers, and are everywhere buoyant and attractive with humour and good humour.'

Fcp. 8vo. boards, Pictorial cover, 2s.; or limp cloth, 2s. 6d.

THE HEIR OF THE AGES.

THE SPECTATOR.—'"The Heir of the Ages" is as pleasant and attractive a story as one can expect to come across.'

THE ATHENÆUM.—'Mr. Payn has always taken a cheerful view of life, but in "The Heir of the Ages" he surpasses himself. . . . Through it all Mr. Payn is at his best.'

THE SCOTSMAN.—'An excellent tale, with some touches in it, as we think, higher than any Mr. Payn has yet attempted.'

THE ACADEMY.—'As bright, as clever, and as interesting as any of its predecessors. In one respect—namely, as regards clear, sympathetic, and graphic delineation of character—it is almost superior to any others by the same writer.'

London: SMITH, ELDER, & CO., 15 Waterloo Place, S.W.

SMITH, ELDER, & CO.'S PUBLICATIONS.

BISMARCK: the Man and the Statesman. Being the Reflections and Reminiscences of Otto, Prince von Bismarck, Written and Dictated by himself after his retirement from office. Translated from the German under the supervision of A. J. BUTLER, late Fellow of Trinity College, Cambridge. With 2 Portraits, Young and Old (Young—from a drawing in the possession of the family; Old—by VON LENBACH), and a Facsimile of Handwriting. 2 vols. Demy 8vo. price 32s.

TIMES (LEADING ARTICLE).—'Of great and enduring interest, and must be read as long as the world continues to interest itself in history and its makers.'

LITERATURE.—'Bismarck's own "Reflections and Recollections" will rank, we think, with that small and select row of books, from the "Commentaries" of Cæsar downwards, in which the chief actors in great affairs have endeavoured to describe their deeds or expound their characters.'

RHODESIA AND ITS GOVERNMENT. By H. C. THOMSON, Author of 'The Chitral Campaign,' and of 'The Outgoing Turk.' With 8 Illustrations and a Map. Large crown 8vo. 10s. 6d.

SPECTATOR.—'We do not hesitate to say that, however fully a man may think himself informed on South African affairs, he will do well to study Mr. Thomson's book. . . . Mr. Thomson's attitude is eminently judicial, and his views are expressed with great moderation. He is in no sense a "crank" or a "faddist."'

THE MUSICIAN'S PILGRIMAGE: a Study in Artistic Development. By J. A. FULLER MAITLAND. Small crown 8vo. 5s.

SPECTATOR.—'We cannot leave this fascinating work without calling attention to the delightful consistency of its construction. The matter of the book is treated with a lucidity and coherence of thought suggestive of the developments of a sonata.'

OUR PRAYER BOOK: CONFORMITY AND CONSCIENCE. By the Rev. W. PAGE ROBERTS, M.A., Canon Residentiary of Canterbury, Author of 'Law and God,' 'Liberalism in Religion,' &c. SECOND EDITION. Crown 8vo. 6s.

ACADEMY.—'The Canon of Canterbury shows with humorous ingenuity that such stumbling blocks as priestly absolution and the unkind threats of the pseudo-Athanasius need constitute no bar to religious communion with the most primitive or the most rationalistic of Puritans.'

INTRODUCTION TO THE STUDY OF THE RENAISSANCE. By Mrs. LILIAN F. FIELD. Crown 8vo. 6s.

ACADEMY.—'Mrs. Field seems to us to have accomplished her difficult task very well. The book is capitally ordered and arranged; the essential is properly kept in the foreground, and the writing is clear, sympathetic, and scholarly.'

THE SEPOY MUTINY, AS SEEN BY A SUBALTERN FROM DELHI TO LUCKNOW. By Col. EDWARD VIBART. With 2 Portraits, a Plan, and 10 Illustrations. Large crown 8vo. 7s. 6d.

ARMY AND NAVY GAZETTE.—'A narrative of surpassing interest. It holds the reader spell-bound by its intensity of feeling and narrative power.'

CHARLES LAMB AND THE LLOYDS. Edited by E. V. LUCAS. With Portraits and a Facsimile Letter. Small post 8vo. 6s.

MANCHESTER GUARDIAN.—'It is difficult to maintain critical composure and decorum on a discovery like this, and the difficulty becomes an impossibility when it is found that these additions to the canon of Lamb's writings are not inferior in beauty and interest to the best of his published work.'

IDLEHURST: a Journal kept in the Country. By JOHN HALSHAM. Crown 8vo. 8s.

PALL MALL GAZETTE.—'Very charming. . . . The best advice we can give to those who like to read about the country is to get "Idlehurst" for themselves.'

THE POETICAL WORKS OF ROBERT BRIDGES. Vols. I. and II. Small crown 8vo. 6s. each.

ACADEMY.—'In this edition Mr. Bridges at once makes his bow to the general public, and at the same time assumes the honours of an established and recognised poet.'

PAGES FROM A PRIVATE DIARY. Reprinted from the *Cornhill Magazine*. FOURTH EDITION. Crown 8vo. 6s.

ATHENÆUM.—'Full of happy sayings, of stories, and of pleasant turns of observation . . . and amusing from cover to cover. . . . Really a model to modern writers of diaries for the public.'

London: SMITH, ELDER, & CO., 15 Waterloo Place, S.W.

SMITH, ELDER, & CO.'S PUBLICATIONS.

THE LETTERS OF ROBERT BROWNING AND ELIZABETH BARRETT BARRETT. THIRD IMPRESSION. With 2 Portraits and 2 Facsimile Letters. 2 vols. Crown 8vo. 21s.

SPECTATOR.—'We venture to think that no such remarkable and unbroken series of intimate letters between two remarkable people has ever been given to the world. . . . There is something extraordinarily touching in the gradual unfolding of the romance in which two poets play the parts of hero and heroine.'

THE ETCHINGHAM LETTERS. By Mrs. FULLER MAITLAND, Author of 'Pages from the Day-Book of Bethia Hardacre,' &c., and Sir FREDERICK POLLOCK, Bart. SECOND IMPRESSION. Crown 8vo. 6s.

LITERATURE.—'The charm of the book lies mainly in that slowly elaborated presentment of character in which no method can rival the epistolary. . . . Every page in the book is pervaded by a charm which one values in proportion to its increasing rarity—the charm of scholarship.'

THE WAR IN CUBA. The Experiences of an Englishman with the United States Army. By JOHN BLACK ATKINS, M.A. With 4 Maps and a Frontispiece. Crown 8vo. 6s.

DAILY CHRONICLE.—'A most vivid and entertaining description, giving us a far better idea of what the war was really like to the men who took part in it than all the possible statistics and military treatises.'

A LIFE OF WILLIAM SHAKESPEARE. By SIDNEY LEE, Editor of 'The Dictionary of National Biography.' FOURTH EDITION. With 2 Portraits of Shakespeare, a Portrait of the Earl of Southampton, and Facsimiles of Shakespeare's known Signatures. Crown 8vo. 7s. 6d.

LITERATURE.—'Mr. Lee's work, both for its literary qualities and its scholarship, does credit to English letters, and it will probably be regarded for years to come as the most useful, the most judicious, and the most authoritative of all existing biographies of the poet.'

SHAKESPEARE'S HANDWRITING. Facsimiles of the Five Authentic Autograph Signatures of the Poet. Extracted from SIDNEY LEE'S 'Life of William Shakespeare.' With an Explanatory Note. Crown 8vo. 6d.

THE CRUISE OF THE 'CACHALOT' ROUND THE WORLD AFTER SPERM WHALES. By FRANK T. BULLEN, First Mate. The Volume includes a Letter to the Author from RUDYARD KIPLING. FOURTH EDITION. With 8 Illustrations and a Chart. Large post 8vo. 8s. 6d.

TIMES.—'Mr. Bullen has a splendid subject, and he handles it with the pen of a master. . . . "The Cruise of the *Cachalot*" is a book which cannot but fascinate all lovers of the sea, and all who can appreciate a masterly presentation of its wonder and its mystery, its terrors and its trials, its humours and its tragedies.'

THE LIFE OF CHARLES STEWART PARNELL (1846-1891). By R. BARRY O'BRIEN, Author of 'Fifty Years of Concessions to Ireland,' &c. THIRD IMPRESSION. With a Portrait, a view of Avondale, and a Facsimile Letter. 2 vols. Large post 8vo. 21s.

THE EARL OF ROSEBERY at Edinburgh.—'The remarkable biography of a remarkable man.'

DAILY CHRONICLE.—'A book which ranks among the great biographies of the century.'

FIGHTS FOR THE FLAG. By W. H. FITCHETT ('VEDETTE'). Author of 'Deeds that Won the Empire.' SECOND EDITION. With 16 Portraits, 13 Plans, and a Facsimile Letter of the Duke of Marlborough. Crown 8vo. 6s.

REVIEW OF REVIEWS.—'This is the second volume of the series which has achieved one of the greatest literary successes of our time. . . . As a gift book, or as a book to take up and read at odd moments, or to devour at a prolonged sitting, this book has few equals.'

By the same Author.

DEEDS THAT WON THE EMPIRE. TENTH EDITION. With 16 Portraits and 11 Plans. Crown 8vo. 6s.

SPECTATOR.—'Not since Macaulay ceased to write has English literature produced a writer capable of infusing such life and vigour into historical scenes. The wholesome and manly tone of Mr. Fitchett's book is specially satisfactory. . . . The book cannot but take the reader by storm wherever it finds him.'

London: SMITH, ELDER, & CO., 15 Waterloo Place, S.W.

POPULAR NOVELS.

Each Work complete in One Volume, crown 8vo. price Six Shillings.

By HENRY SETON MERRIMAN:
  RODEN'S CORNER. 3rd Edition.
  IN KEDAR'S TENTS. 8th Edition.
  THE GREY LADY. With 12 Full-page Illustrations.
  THE SOWERS. 19th Edition.

By A. CONAN DOYLE:
  THE TRAGEDY OF THE KOROSKO. With 40 Full-page Illustrations.
  UNCLE BERNAC. 2nd Edition. With 12 Full-page Illustrations.
  RODNEY STONE. With 8 Full-page Illustrations.
  THE WHITE COMPANY. 20th Edition.

By S. R. CROCKETT:
  THE BLACK DOUGLAS. With 8 Full-page Illustrations. 2nd Edition.
  THE RED AXE. With 8 Full-page Illustrations. 3rd Edition.
  CLEG KELLY, ARAB OF THE CITY. 3rd Edition.

By Mrs. HUMPHRY WARD:
  HELBECK OF BANNISDALE. 5th Edition.
  SIR GEORGE TRESSADY. 4th Edition.
  MARCELLA. 16th Edition.
  ROBERT ELSMERE. 27th Edition.
  THE HISTORY OF DAVID GRIEVE. 9th Edition.

By STANLEY J. WEYMAN:
  THE CASTLE INN. With a Frontispiece. 4th Edition.

By Miss THACKERAY:
  OLD KENSINGTON.
  THE VILLAGE ON THE CLIFF.
  FIVE OLD FRIENDS AND A YOUNG PRINCE.
  TO ESTHER, and other Sketches.
  BLUEBEARD'S KEYS, and other Stories.
  THE STORY OF ELIZABETH; TWO HOURS; FROM AN ISLAND.
  TOILERS AND SPINSTERS; and other Essays.
  MISS ANGEL: Fulham Lawn.
  MISS WILLIAMSON'S DIVAGATIONS.
  MRS. DYMOND.

By CLIVE PHILLIPPS-WOLLEY:
  ONE OF THE BROKEN BRIGADE.

By ALEXANDER INNES SHAND:
  THE LADY GRANGE.

By the Rev. J. E. C. WELLDON:
  GERALD EVERSLEY'S FRIENDSHIP: a Study in Real Life. 4th Edition.

By G. COLMORE:
  THE STRANGE STORY OF HESTER WYNNE. 2nd Impression.

By K. and HESKETH PRICHARD (E. & H. HERON):
  A MODERN MERCENARY.

By JOHN GARRETT LEIGH:
  GOD'S GREETING.

By KATHARINE TYNAN:
  SHE WALKS IN BEAUTY.
  THE DEAR IRISH GIRL. 3rd Edition.

By Sir WM. MAGNAY, Bart.
  THE HEIRESS OF THE SEASON
  THE PRIDE OF LIFE.

By the Vicomte JEAN DE LUZ:
  MA MÈRE; or Sons and Daughters under the Second Empire.

By ARCHIE ARMSTRONG:
  UNDER THE CIRCUMSTANCES

By the Rev. COSMO GORDON LANG:
  THE YOUNG CLANROY: Romance of the '45.

By W. CARLTON DAWE:
  CAPTAIN CASTLE: a Story of the South Sea. With a Frontispiece.

By Mrs. DE LA PASTURE:
  ADAM GRIGSON.
  DEBORAH OF TOD'S. 4th Edition.

By ANNA HOWARTH:
  SWORD AND ASSEGAI.
  JAN: an Afrikander. 2nd Edition.
  KATRINA: a Tale of the Karoo.

By FRANCIS H. HARDY:
  THE MILLS OF GOD.

By HAMILTON DRUMMOND:
  FOR THE RELIGION.

By ARCHER P. CROUCH:
  SEÑORITA MONTENAR.

By J. A. ALTSHELER:
  A SOLDIER OF MANHATTAN.

By OLIVE BIRRELL:
  THE AMBITION OF JUDITH.

By Mrs. BIRCHENOUGH:
  DISTURBING ELEMENTS.

By LORD MONKSWELL:
  KATE GRENVILLE.

By SARAH TYTLER:
  KINCAID'S WIDOW.

London: SMITH, ELDER, & CO., 15 Waterloo Place, S.W.

www.ingramcontent.com/pod-product-compliance
Lightning Source LLC
Chambersburg PA
CBHW032131230426
43672CB00011B/2302